To our Gregory
Merry Christmas 1996
with love
Mom and Dad

Look for your name and your friends on the end pages or visit our website at http://www.cyber24.com

**"Every time a new user arrives,
the whole Net
gets more valuable to everyone on it."**
—Marc Andreessen

You are about to enter a digital time capsule, an extraordinary collection of photographs taken on a single, ordinary day— Thursday, February 8, 1996. These images, captured by 150 photojournalists dispatched to every continent, record how the online world is changing our lives. No picture here is more than 24 hours older or younger than any other. And every photograph was shot for a single purpose: to document the harmonies and paradoxes of life in cyberspace as it was lived on this one day.

Cyberspace is no longer an abstraction; it is now the real world—the marketplace, the battleground, the house of prayer, the secret retreat. It is a place where we meet, and to which we venture alone. It's as comfortable and as boundless as the street where we live, as wondrous and frightening as the first day of kindergarten. We have yet to reach the borders of this brand- new place, and we may well discover that it has none. In fact, on the day this project took place, controversial legislation was signed into law that threatens the very freedom of speech the Net has come to nurture.

There are hundreds of photographs in this book, selected from the more than 200,000 shot on February 8. But even 200,000 images barely hint at the infinite moments that passed through the hills and homes and hearts of humanity on that day. On February 8, 1996, cyberspace was frozen in time, and for decades to come, our children and our children's children will look with wonder at this photographic record of an ordinary day when millions of people around the planet took the time to paint their own names on the walls of the digital cave. ■

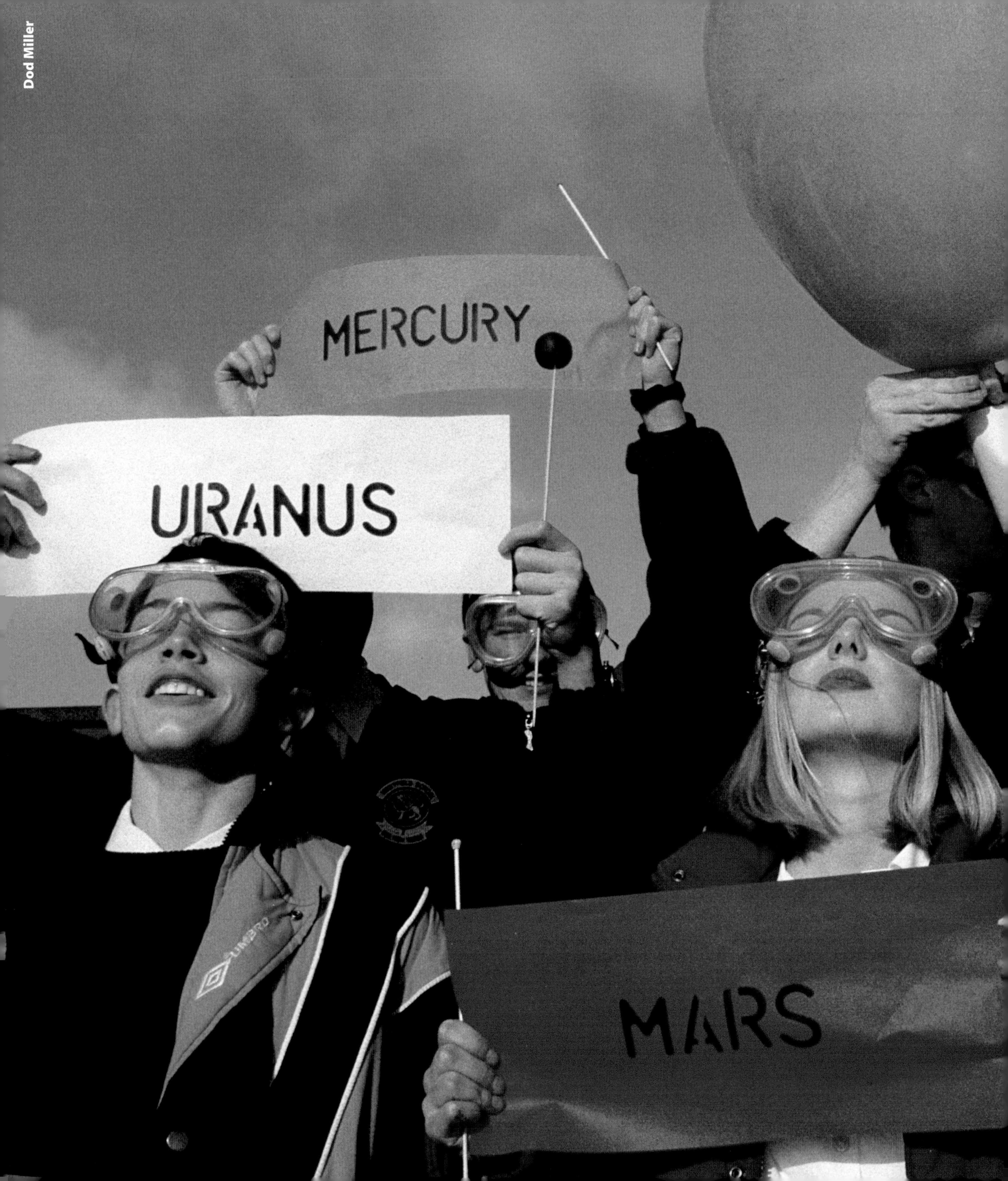

Dod Miller

24 Hours in Cyberspace *was made possible*
through the generous sponsorship of the following companies:

www.kodak.com

www.adobe.com

www.sun.com

www.aol.com

www.netscape.com

MFS Communications

Power Computing

Illustra

NEC Technologies

NetObjects

Studio Archetype

A&I Color

24 Hours in Cyberspace

Photographed on one day by 150 of the world's leading photojournalists

Created by Rick Smolan and Jennifer Erwitt

Produced by Against All Odds Productions

A Nick Harris Book
SOMERVILLE HOUSE PUBLISHING
TORONTO

CREDITS

Project Directors
Rick Smolan
Jennifer Erwitt

COO and Technical Director
Tom Melcher

Director of Photography and Assignments
Karen Mullarkey

Art Director and Designer
Lori Barra

Writer
Eileen Matthews Hansen

Vice President, Publicity
Patti Richards

Marketing and Student Underground Coordinator
Gina Privitere

ISBN: 1-895897-80-7

A Nick Harris Book

Published by Somerville House Publishing,
a division of Somerville House Books Limited,
3080 Yonge Street, Suite 5000, Toronto, Ontario M4N 3N1
E-mail address: sombooks@goodmedia.com
Website: http://www.goodmedia.com/somervillehouse

Simultaneously published by Against All Odds Productions, USA

Somerville House Publishing acknowledges the financial assistance of the Ontario Publishing Centre, the Ontario Arts Council, the Ontario Development Corporation, and the Department of Communications.

Petri Kurkaa

Human Touch Reaching, Finding, Holding

18 *People are going online to find things they may not have found IRL (in real life). The virtual community brings together people of like minds who were once separated by geography. Stories range from an AIDS quilt cybermemorial to a wounded soldier in Bosnia, whose plea for help was answered on the Net.*

Misha Erwitt

Open for Business No Paper, No Printing, No Postage

116 *The Internet is revolutionizing boardrooms from New York to New Delhi. The democratic world of the Web allows small businesses with limited budgets to serve customers anywhere on the planet. This section contains stories of mom-and-pop startups, blue-chip corporations, and intrepid individuals from every nation who have stepped through this new door of opportunity.*

Contents

Eugene Fisher

Jim Gensheimer

Peter Charlesworth

Andy Levin

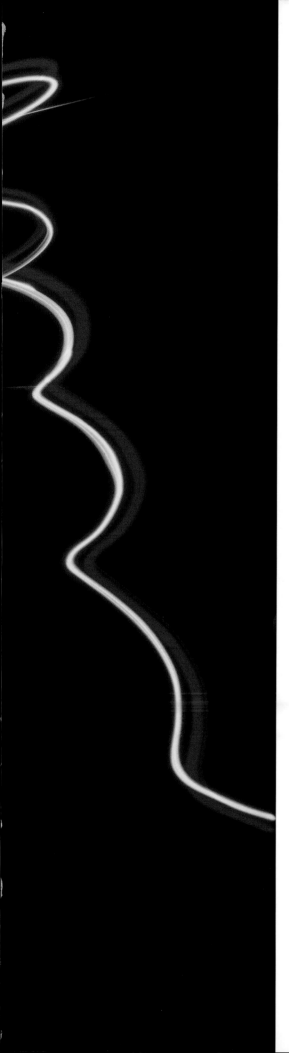

Preface by Paul Saffo

Director, Institute for the Future

Thirty years ago, a handful of Pentagon-funded computer wizards laid the foundation for what would become the Internet. Armageddon was in the air, so they constructed their mind-child with a peculiar architecture designed to scurry data around even as cities in the Midwest were reduced to clouds of atomic aerosol. But like the interstate highway system of the 1950s—designed so the military could shuttle missiles around the country, making these targets ever movable—features designed for war proved even more valuable in the unexpected peace that followed. The Beat generation was born on the interstate, while the Internet's architecture made it singularly amenable to reinvention into something utterly unanticipated by its creators or their warlord patrons.

For most people, the Internet is more of a medium than a technology. Moreover, it is a shape-shifting, borderless medium firmly in the hands of ordinary citizens bent on turning it to extraordinary ends. Revolution *has* become commonplace in our vocabulary, and so the real thing is often hard to recognize. But the stories told in this book and in its companion website make it clear that nothing less is afoot on the Internet today. From Inuit children doing their homework to Benedictine monks selling monastic fruitcake, this is the stuff of deep innovation and change. This is the domain of real people discovering new possibilities on the frontiers of cyberspace.

Yet, compelling as these stories may be, the changes have barely begun. The Internet is passing through an awkward adolescence, rebellious and plagued by gawky interfaces, too-slow access times, and more than its share of pointless banality. Despite these growing pains, the Internet is already more representative of our global diversity and more important to our collective future than the passive medium of television.

Ahead is all surprise, frustrating for those attached to the status quo but welcome to world changers and wizards. If we all participate, the result could well be a widening of the human spirit and the creation of a new home for the mind. Recall a question posed by C.S. Lewis decades ago: "Will you be the child courting the spell or the magician casting it?" Read on, and the answer will become clear.

Human Touch

Countries
represented:

Australia

Bosnia

Cambodia

Croatia

England

Estonia

Israel

Turkey

USA

◀ **Annapolis, Maryland, USA**

Last year, Barry Conner and his 11-year-old son, Brent, shared a hug—for the first time. Like many suffering from autism, Brent finds touch highly disturbing, and his moods are erratic. The world is a confusing place for Brent, and doubly so for his parents, whose other son also is autistic. The Conners found a local support group, but without child care, attending meetings was impossible. Luckily, Conner discovered an online mailing list about autism hosted by Carolyn Baird (see next page). "It's a tremendous support," says Conner. "Sometimes just an 'I've been there' comment on the list lifts me out of potential despair."

Photograph by Michael Bryant

The source of cyberspace's obsessive appeal isn't technology or information but people. In fact, it is really an interpersonal medium in which information plays a supporting role. As the stories in this chapter show, cybercitizens aren't introverts engaged in the solitary pursuit of arcane knowledge, but real people interacting with other real people around common interests and concerns. A request for advice, a cry for help, an invitation to play: Desires like these and their satisfaction are at the very heart of the online revolution today.

Cyberspace has become a globe-girdling digital amplifier for human touch, a vehicle for linking people around the globe into new kinds of communities that transcend time and space. Parents laboring alone to raise autistic children discover each other on the Net, trade insights, and become sources of mutual support. Similar stories are emerging everywhere, as people who would never have met in the physical world encounter one another online and build deep human bonds.

Cyberspace is also an amplifier for the full range of human possibility, from love and commitment to common cause. Strangers communing in cyberspace have toppled politicians and caused corporations to retreat from seemingly fixed policies. Aided by volunteers at Yale University, Cambodian prosecutors are traversing cyberspace, seeking out witnesses against the Khmer perpetrators of the infamous killing fields.

These communities are unlike traditional communities in important ways. Often they are more volatile, converging overnight around a common hot issue and then evaporating once the issue is resolved. But the biggest difference is that the medium of interaction is electronic, and members may never actually meet each other in person. For the uninitiated, this seems an insurmountable obstacle to creating "real" communities. However, the stories in this chapter make it clear that when delivered instantly online, even text alone can be sufficient to build community and commitment.

In the end, electronic and conventional communities will merge into a larger whole. It is already happening, for electronic friendships inevitably lead to face-to-face meetings, and conversations begun in person are increasingly continued online. It will not be long before cyberspace becomes an unremarkable and invisible extension of human touch.—P.S.

◀ **Newcastle, Australia**

Affectionately known as "Mummy HFA" (short for "Mummy high-functioning autistic"), Carolyn Baird is the mother of four autistic children and the host of an autism-related mailing list.

Baird has always been keenly aware of the subtle differences between herself and others. For years, she struggled with her own inexplicable and inappropriate behavior. Research on the Internet led her to discover the many forms that autism can take. Relieved—finally—to have a label for the problem that plagues her and her children, Baird resolved to share her experiences via the Internet. Today her mailing list links autistics in far-flung countries, from Egypt and France to the United States. For many members, the contact has meant the difference between suffering in silence and finding comfort in others. "The response to my first post was truly the turning point in my life," says Baird. "Through the mailing list I finally met other high-functioning autistic people and immediately felt right at home—I'd found my lost tribe."

Photograph by Petri Kurkaa

▲ **Carolyn Baird with her four children, ages nine to 25. Her oldest son, Chris, a high-functioning autistic like his mother, has met all of his friends via the Internet.**

▲ ▶ **Linking Lusk to cyberspace stirs hopes of rebirth. Here, schoolchildren take 103-year-old Ocea Liss on a digital tour. County researcher Lisa Shaw (right) collects information for a statewide database, which local ranchers will use to determine grazing patterns.**

Lusk, Wyoming, USA

Build it and they will come. That's the dream in Lusk, a town of 1,504 that has staked its future on the Internet. Armed with a $290,000 state grant, Lusk persuaded US West to hook it up to the Net via a new fiber-optics line; it also installed a cable system connecting City Hall, the hospital, two schools, and 600 homes. The result: Once threatened with economic extinction, today Lusk is a rare combination of high technology and low living costs. That formula has already attracted two companies to town, including one that makes electronic components for security gates at the White House. Mayor Donald Whiteaker says the Internet is a lot like the railroad that once made Lusk boom. "I can't attract [jobs] if I don't have a highway," says Whiteaker. "If you build it and nobody comes, that's their problem. But I know for sure they won't come if it isn't built." *Photographs by Lynn Johnson*

▲ **Brooklyn, New York, USA**

Maurice Ashley, America's first African-American international chess master, says the game got him through his teenage years in a rough section of Brooklyn. As part of the Chess in the Schools program, sponsored by the American Chess Foundation, 29-year-old Ashley acts as an online coach for kids in inner-city schools across the country. According to Yvette LeWinter, a teacher at Valerio Street School in Van Nuys, California, the program has helped her third-grade students develop critical-thinking and social skills. "The program has been a savior for kids with discipline problems. They're learning to play fairly and to get along with others," says LeWinter. Ashley sees the program as mutually beneficial: "Now I can relate to kids 3,000 miles away and see them grow as a result. It's mind-blowing."

Photograph by Andy Levin

▲ Austin, Texas, USA

When artist Layne Jackson logs on to the Web, her screen fills with questions— honest, searching questions—from adolescent girls all over the country. "How did you know you were an artist?" "How will I know if I'm artist?" As an online mentor for Girl Games, a company developing software and Internet activities for girls, Jackson fields questions, gives advice, and strives to inspire her "mentees" to take a chance and explore the options available to them—including technology. For Jackson, the medium is as powerful as the message. "Lots of girls are shy and afraid to ask questions or voice their opinions, but I find the Internet gives them the space and freedom to let their ideas flow."
Photograph by Larry Price

Emma Lawrence, 10, meets with online mentor and artist Layne Jackson (left) in Layne's studio. The two met on the Net as part of the Girl Games mentoring program.

▲ **Charlotte, North Carolina, USA**

Caregiving came full circle for online AIDS worker Debbi Hood Johnson. Johnson first reached out to the Internet for help when her husband, B.J. Johnson, died of AIDS. "I had isolated myself from our circle of friends and was really keening for him," recalled Johnson. Realizing that cyberspace offered a safe haven, she contacted the Computer AIDS Ministry, a New York BBS. Soon, sympathetic strangers became supportive friends. Johnson, who had been trained as an AIDS educator, began answering questions on an adult-oriented BBS. A year later, she learned that she, too, was HIV-positive. Once again, she found herself on the receiving end of the support system. *Epilogue:* Johnson died in a car accident on February 24, just 16 days after this photo was taken.
Photograph by Gary O'Brien

▶ **San Francisco, California, USA**

Like the epidemic itself, the AIDS Memorial Quilt has become a burden that is almost too heavy to carry. Beginning as a few rectangles stitched together in 1989 to commemorate some of the early victims of AIDS, the quilt has grown to 33,000 panels, each a portrait of the lives and loves of someone lost to AIDS. Together, the panels cover an astonishing 14 acres and weigh 38 tons. Displaying the quilt is a job that requires thousands of volunteers and countless hours of folding and unfolding. Consequently, full displays of the quilt are rare, and take place only in Washington, D.C. But now The Names Project Foundation, which maintains the quilt, has begun a digital archive that will record each panel and display it electronically—in all its sad glory—for those who want a glimpse of the true toll of AIDS. Volunteer George Renz (right) repairs a worn panel in preparation for archiving.
Photograph by Acey Harper

"This is for women of the African Diaspora, all over the planet."

—Eno Jackson

◀ **Roxbury, Massachusetts, USA**

As an African-American woman among hundreds of white male graduate students at the Massachusetts Institute of Technology, Eno Jackson knew what it was like to feel isolated. Realizing that her situation was far from unique, she sought a way to connect with others in similar circumstances. Her solution? A website dedicated to information of interest to African-American women. Jackson's Isis site links to other sites covering African and African-American literature, art, and culture. It also contains a wealth of historical material that she found while searching the Internet for obscure memoirs and chronicles about black women. The response has been tremendous. "I was shocked to discover that I had more than 8,000 hits in one month," says Jackson. "Now I hear every day from other black women who tell me they feel affirmed and inspired by the Isis pages."
Photograph by Stan Grossfeld

▲ **Zagreb, Croatia**

Now that the Iron Curtain has fallen, financier George Soros is lifting the Information Curtain that cloaks Eastern Europe. Last year, his Open Society Institute's Regional Internet Program set up electronic bulletin boards in Bosnia and Herzegovina, a medical Internet node for 20 Slovakian hospitals, and low-cost connectivity at private organizations and schools in Czechoslovakia and the republic of Georgia. Soros vows to continue his efforts until open societies exist everywhere: "I have devoted exactly half my income and a substantially larger portion of my time and energy to my foundation network," he says. *Photograph by Filip Horvat*

▶ **Sarajevo, Bosnia**

With Soros' help, American Eric Bachman, 47, started Zamir Transnational Net, the only email link between the former Yugoslavia and the world. After a recent blast in Sarajevo that killed 37 people, Bachman emailed his sister in America: "I am fine," it read, but **"several shells exploded very near. Life and death continue here."** *Photograph by Wesley Bocxe*

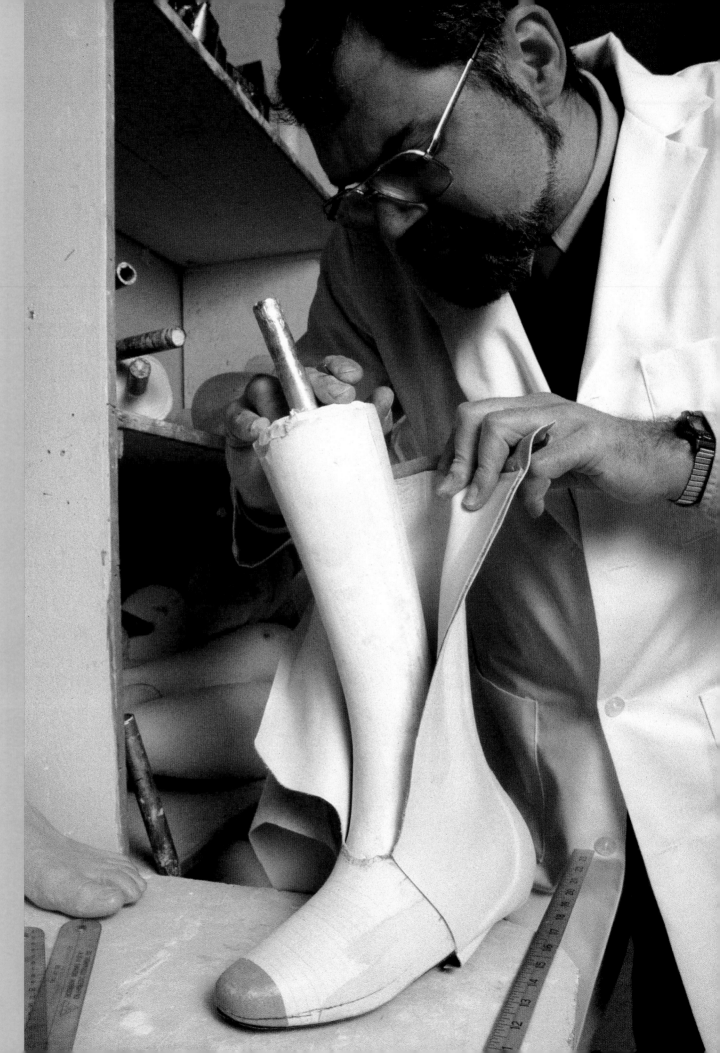

Using an email
support network
that spanned
the globe and
overcame com-
munication barriers,
Dan McNamara
was able to create
a new foot for
Bosno Zijad, an
injured soldier in
Sarajevo.

▲ Sarajevo, Bosnia

"My name is Bosno Zijad. I am a student, male, age 29. I live in Sarajevo and for the last three years I was in Bosnian army. On October 11, 1994, I was wounded and lost my foot. This opportunity I call all people who can help, or give me information for my problem. I will not cry or beg for someone's understanding. I only call all good people who want to help me get back again to normal life."—*Email sent via Zamir Transnational Net, May 4, 1995*
Photograph by Steve Ringman

◀ Olympia, Washington, USA

Thanks to Zamir Transnational Net, Dan McNamara, a prosthetics technician in the United States, made a virtual house call to Bosnia. For McNamara, working across international borders was nothing new. In 1993, he used a rough tracing from New Guinea to create a prosthesis for a boy there. But in the case of Bosno Zijad, a soldier in war-torn Sarajevo, precise measurements were harder to come by. "I wondered how I could get the information rapidly," says McNamara. But the Net offered a new way. Via email, McNamara told Zijad how to make a cast impression of his foot. Soon it arrived, nestled in a cardboard box. McNamara then used the cast as the model for a new prosthesis. A few months later, Zijad's new foot was on its way to Sarajevo.
Photograph by Wesley Bocxe

◀ ▲ **Phnom Penh, Cambodia**

Who were the millions killed by Cambodia's Khmer Rouge, and why has no one been indicted for these atrocities? The Cambodian Genocide Program promises answers to these haunting questions. Begun in 1995 by the U.S. Congress and run from Yale University, the program is creating online catalogs of the extensive evidence the Khmer Rouge left behind, including torture manuals, massacre orders, and photos of victims just before execution. At the Cambodia Documentation Center (above), images of the dead line the walls. Soon the scanned images will go online. A blank area beneath the picture will provide space for the victim's name. The hope is that friends or relatives will come forth and identify the dead. Armed with that evidence, perhaps the perpetrators of one of the most chilling episodes in history will eventually be brought to justice.
Photographs (above and preceding pages) by Darren Whiteside

▶ **Boston, Massachusetts, USA**

Joseph Roger O'Dell is on death row for a murder he claims he didn't commit. With authorities at Mecklenburg Correctional Center in Boydton, Virginia, blocking his access to reporters, O'Dell took to cyberspace, using a Web page created by Boston law student Lori Urs to lobby for a new trial. Urs says the information posted on the website raises important questions about the DNA evidence used to convict O'Dell in 1986. Meanwhile, others have gone online to protest their innocence: Girvies L. Davies, an illiterate burglar convicted of killing an Illinois farmer in 1978, had his own Web page but was executed last year. And more than 100 Web pages and newsgroups have sprung up in the case of Mumia Abu-Jamal, a black journalist convicted of killing a white Philadelphia policeman. *Epilogue:* O'Dell remains on death row, and an execution date has not been set.
Photograph by Steve Krongard

▲ Boulder,
Colorado, USA

"I want to find out
what kind of place
the Net really is.
Do people with big
hearts ever
frequent the Net?"
—*Ed Arnold*
*Photograph by
Paul Chesley*

▶ Tallin, Estonia

**Young and gifted, Aul Pedajas is in danger
of being committed to a nursing institu-
tion for the rest of his life.** At 32, Pedajas
already speaks six languages, holds degrees in
math and computers, and has represented
Estonia at international conferences for the
disabled. But he suffers from spinal muscular
atrophy, a genetic disorder that has trapped
his brilliant mind in a degenerating body.
With no family and an income of only $300 a
month, Pedajas can't afford the full-time care
he needs to live on his own. The alternative is
a nursing home, a place where Pedajas says he
would feel "buried alive." Last year, Pedajas
made a last-ditch plea for help on the
Internet. Across the globe, Ed Arnold (above,
with daughter Johanna), a 49-year-old
programmer and parent of a disabled child,
heard his cry. Arnold found Pedajas' message
while researching the Web for information
related to his daughter's condition. Arnold
created a Web page seeking financial and legal
support for Pedajas; response was strong at
first, but has since dwindled. A discouraged
Arnold vows to press on. "I want to find out
what kind of place the Net really is," he says.
"The situation with Aul piqued my curiosity.
Rather than using the Net for technological
prowess or marketing, would it be possible to
use it for higher reasons? Do people with big
hearts ever frequent the Net?"
Photograph by Joey Abraityte

◀ **Yorkshire, England**

At 27, David Winder suddenly found himself at rock bottom. His wild days on the streets of London were cut short by encephalitis, an illness that left him wheelchair-bound and speech-impaired. His family life was shattered. Facing unbearable bleakness, Winder attempted suicide twice and turned to drugs and drink for solace. To help lift him out of his depression, a friend gave Winder a used computer and connected him to the Internet. The moment Winder went online, he saw a chance to reinvent himself. Finding an audience more interested in his ideas than his appearance, Winder became Wavy Davy, leader of a new underground culture that he keeps alive through gritty weekly Web columns and newsgroups. Winder now has 10 books on cyberculture to his credit. But more important, he has a new lease on life. "The Net gave me a role in the world at a time when I thought I didn't have one," says Winder.

Photograph by Dario Mitidieri

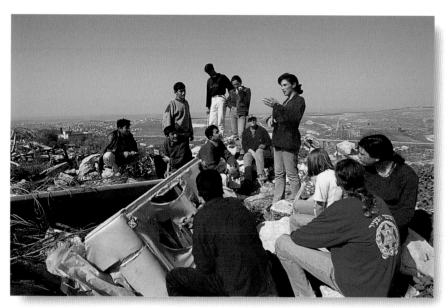

▲ Chadera, Israel

Arab and Israeli teens connect online as part of The Living Weave, a community-based project that sponsors intervillage chats between high-school students.
Photograph by Ricki Rosen

▶ **Kiryat Sefer, Israel**

Tzadik Vanderhoof (right) studies the Talmud with a fellow settlement member. In the background: Tzadik's wife, Sheva, and son—and breaking news from CNN's website.
Photograph by Ricki Rosen

In a country where political and religious issues fill the air as frequently as gunfire, cyberspace offers a safe haven where people can share information, unhindered by partisan beliefs. When Israeli Prime Minister Yitzak Rabin was assassinated in Tel Aviv, about 30 miles from the home of Tzadik and Sheva Vanderhoof, they were unaware of the tragedy until they received an email from a relative in Canada, 5,000 miles away. As residents of a small settlement of orthodox Jews located in the Israeli-occupied West Bank, the Vanderhoofs are allowed to get their information only through orthodox Hebrew-language papers. Televisions are banned in the settlement, and newspapers often are censored. Ex-New Yorkers used to getting the news of the world, the Vanderhoofs hungered for outside information. Fortunately, Tzadik's job gives them access to a computer. Through the Internet, they can keep in touch with friends and relatives around the world and log on to the CNN Interactive website to monitor political events—even those in their own backyard.

"Cyberspace answered our need for a safe, nonconfrontational milieu."

—Deb Dvir, cofounder of The Living Weave

▲ ▶ **Blacksburg, Virginia, USA**

It's the most wired town in America—but will the Internet really pull Blacksburg, Virginia, closer together? The question worries some in this small town (population 35,000) nestled in the Blue Ridge Mountains. Home to Virginia Polytechnic Institute, Blacksburg was once rated one of America's top 20 places to retire—a place where the Lions Club and student hangouts mix comfortably. But appearances are deceiving: Next to the pretty churches is an electronic mall, populated by 150 businesses. Thanks to the Blacksburg Electronic Village Project, a joint venture including Bell Atlantic, 40 percent of Blacksburg's citizens have Internet access, and 14,000 email subscribers receive 110,000 messages a day. Apply for a credit card, order a pizza, rent an apartment, check out a video—all online. Not surprisingly, there are critics; one local therapist fears that "the electronic village will further erode the real village." But technology has many faces: The local Habitat for Humanity is using the Web to help turn a historic church into a new home for a poor family.
Photographs by Randy Olson

Harvey Hicks, 76, is one of the last living members of a historic church built by freed slaves, which is being renovated as a new home for a local family.

▲ Swarthmore, Pennsylvania, USA

"Folks connect with honesty. Intentions come through in the speed of the surf. This may be a new medium, but I got old messages—be yourself, feel the force, and share alike." On Justin Hall's website, Links from the Underground, matters of life, love, and culture spill down the page like a wired version of beat poetry. Hall, 21, started writing for the Web two years ago—"I did it because it was fun," he says. "I wasn't trying to carve out a digital niche"—but two years later, his page has garnered some 200,000 hits. Now Hall is a rising star. "Guys with suits and too much money came and started asking me about 'content providing' and 'youth culture'—like I've found the philosopher's stone of neglect," he says. Instead he's taking the low road, planning a summer bus tour with stops in various cities, where he'll teach others how to write their own Web pages. Along with cyberspace, self-publishing is Hall's passion: "I've got oodles of love to give back to the Net."
Photograph by Sarah Leen

▲ **Istanbul, Turkey**

In September 1993, 21-year-old Tolga Yurderi played the role of electronic carrier pigeon, relaying a message from the besieged Russian Republic of Georgia to the United Nations. The message was desperate. It was sent by a group of women who retrieved Yurderi's email address from his correspondence with scientists at the Georgian space research center. The country was under siege by Abkhazian rebels backed by Russian extremists. All phone lines had been cut. But via the Internet—which originated as a backup communications system in the event of a direct nuclear attack—the women knew they could reach someone who might help. Yurderi played good cyber-Samaritan and forwarded the message to the United Nations. Though Georgia still simmers, Yurderi is convinced the Internet can get the word out when all else fails. "You can see from my experience that the Net can make a difference in the world," he says.

Photograph by Sedat Aral

Tolga Yurderi (second from left), leading cybercitizen of Istanbul and now president of his own Internet-based company, meets here with friends at a traditional Turkish bathhouse.

Earthwatch

Countries
represented:

Argentina
Brazil
Canada
China
Egypt
England
Italy
Malaysia
Mexico
Russia
Siberia
USA

◀ **San Antonio, Texas, USA**

Eight chimpanzees were slated for medical testing. Animal-rights activist Carilyn Bucher didn't have the $126,000 needed to save them—but she did have a modem. The chimps' owners had agreed to let the former circus animals retire at Primarily Primates, a Texas sanctuary. But there was a catch: Either come up with the cash to build a chimp shelter, or forfeit the animals. So Bucher took the cause of the "Buckshire Eight" to the Web. Within weeks, calls and cash flooded in. One man offered to sell his baseball-card collection; a woman volunteered to forgo Christmas presents. Today, courtesy of wired animal lovers worldwide, the chimps are alive and well.
Photograph by Larry Price

unta Arenas, Chile, is one of the most remote locations on the planet. When an ozone hole appeared over this town at the very tip of South America in the late 1980s, researchers traveled for days to be on site. On the Internet, Punta Arenas—and research on the ozone hole—is accessible by everyone from scientists to schoolchildren.

Cyberspace is more than a medium for accessing information and other people. It is also an extraordinarily potent tool for seeing our planet in new ways. A decade ago, kids could only read about geography or watch the occasional video. Today, they can "teleport" via the Internet to the ends of the earth and literally look over the shoulders of scientists as they go about their work. Our horizons stretch outward as well, through new electronic windows on the universe. Net surfers are welcome to control a robotic telescope in Bradford, England, or view comets and other planetary wanderers seconds after their images are captured.

But cyberspace does more than demolish remoteness in the service of planetary discovery. It also compresses time. Students in a Michigan classroom interact instantaneously with archeologists in Egypt. Italian cavers once revised their paper-based exploration maps annually; now the maps are updated weekly on the Internet, and the consequence is a dramatic acceleration in the pace of discovery and understanding.

This real-time effect is shrinking our planet. Events halfway around the globe become backyard concerns when we learn of them in real time. Dry facts become living events. Scientists the world over are receiving feeds from a lonely Internet research node in the Amazon. Technologies created for the military are now used to track whales and even an errant Malaysian elephant, thus saving it from almost certain death. And schoolchildren nationwide have become nature watchers by following the migration of butterflies across a continent.

As the planet shrinks, our worldview expands. "Earthwatching" through the lens of cyberspace reveals a place vastly richer, more complex, and more subtle than our predecessors ever imagined. And because the revelations arrive in real time, we can do more than just watch. Online-enabled earthwatchers can also be world changers.—P.S.

Gugliemo de' Micheli

◀ ▲ **Wadi Natrun, Egypt**

Hours from Cairo, an archeologist toils beneath the burning sun, carefully unearthing ancient pottery. Nearby, a bedouin family looks on. Thousands of miles away in Michigan, students gasp in wonder. As part of Odyssey in Egypt, an online archeology project, students can work "virtually" alongside archeologists as they excavate a fourth-century Coptic Monastery. "It puts the trowel in their hands," says Dr. Scott Carroll, head of the excavation. Weekly emails from on-site archeologists cover everything from the dig's progress to information on life in and around the site. The 10-week curriculum also includes emails from a Coptic monk (preceding pages), who lives as a hermit in a cave near the site. *Photographs by Guglielmo de' Micheli*

▲ **Grand Haven, Michigan, USA**

"This is so exciting for me because we're in contact with people who are digging up these artifacts right now," writes Basil Torchin of the Zeeland Middle School. He is not alone. For many students, the Odyssey project is the first time they've ventured online; for all of them, the project's unique blend of remote learning and classroom activities has brought new life to subjects once limited to dry textbooks. Here, a student logs on in his makeshift dig tent. Back at the site in Wadi Natrun, Dr. Carroll's children, B.J., 13, and Ben, 15, act as correspondents, answering email questions sent in by students around the country. In week three of the Odyssey project, B.J. wrote, "Finding stuff hundreds of years old is great. When you find things, you think, 'Wow! A monk who is dead made this pot! He was so careful, and now I'm the first person to have touched it after him!'" *Photograph by J. Kyle Keener*

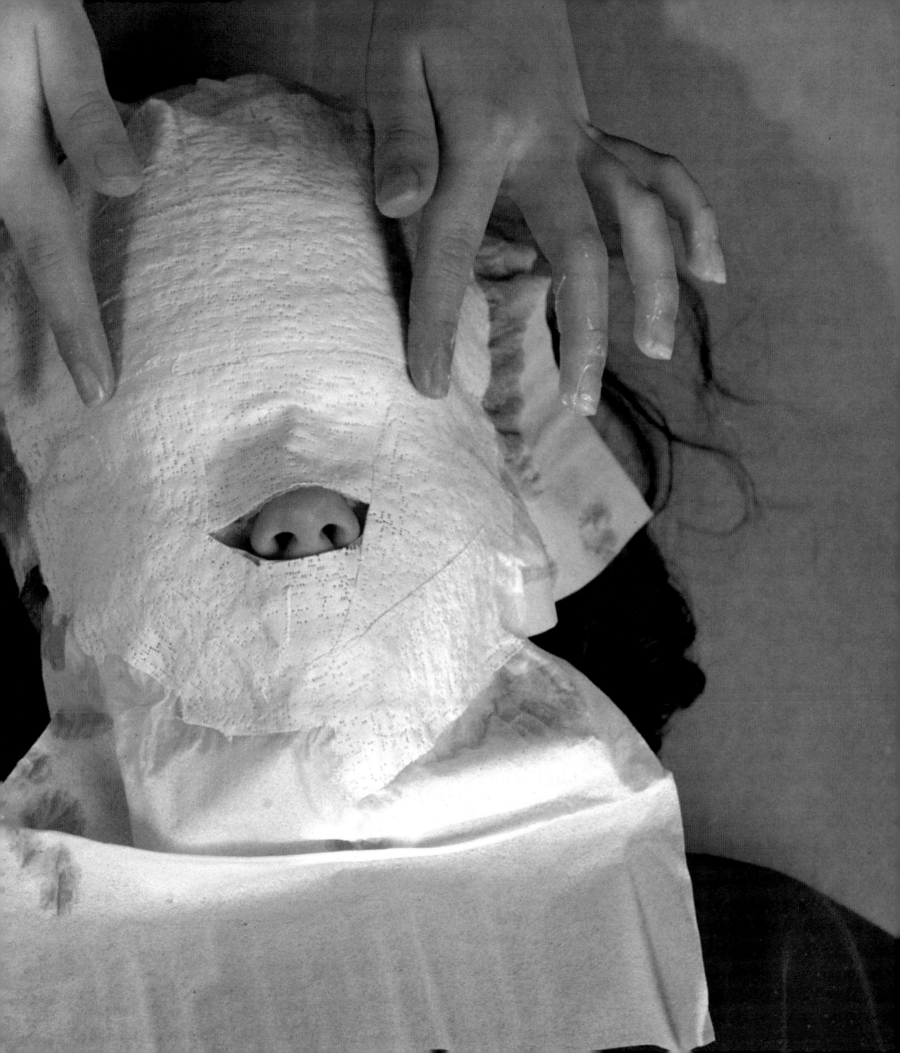

◀ **In a chain of learning that connects two continents via cyberspace, students in Michigan bring online knowledge to hands-on projects such as making a mummy mask or identifying archeological finds.**

▲ **Grand Haven, Michigan, USA**

A piece of pottery is unearthed in Egypt; its image goes online. An offline replica is made, and within days, students hold the discovery in their hands. Whether the hands-on exercise is in the ancient art of mummification (preceding pages) or in the painstaking process of piecing together pottery shards, the goal of Odyssey in Egypt is to make the archeological experience as real as possible. "Sometimes the only thing that students have to go on is the *Indiana Jones* idea," says Steven Boggess, codeveloper of the program. "We wanted to show the real work—and joy—of taking part in a dig." *Photographs by J. Kyle Keener*

▲ Wadi Natrun, Egypt

"We have begun to dig out a small room....
The question still remains: What is a room
doing this high up inside of the wall? It
may be some sort of watch room or a
guard's chamber ... " —*Odyssey in Egypt*
During the Odyssey project, students are
invited to send in their ideas on archeological
finds or dig-site dilemmas. Every week, study
questions are posted on the project's Web
page: What would you do if your dig mate
was stung by a scorpion? How much water a
day would be needed to hydrate 110 dig-site
workers? The online program has been a huge
success. "This has changed the way I think
about social studies," says Michigan student
Allison Haney. Fellow classmate Leigha
Drexler agrees: "It's cool that an 11-year-old
can take advantage of such an awesome thing!"
Photograph by Guglielmo de' Micheli

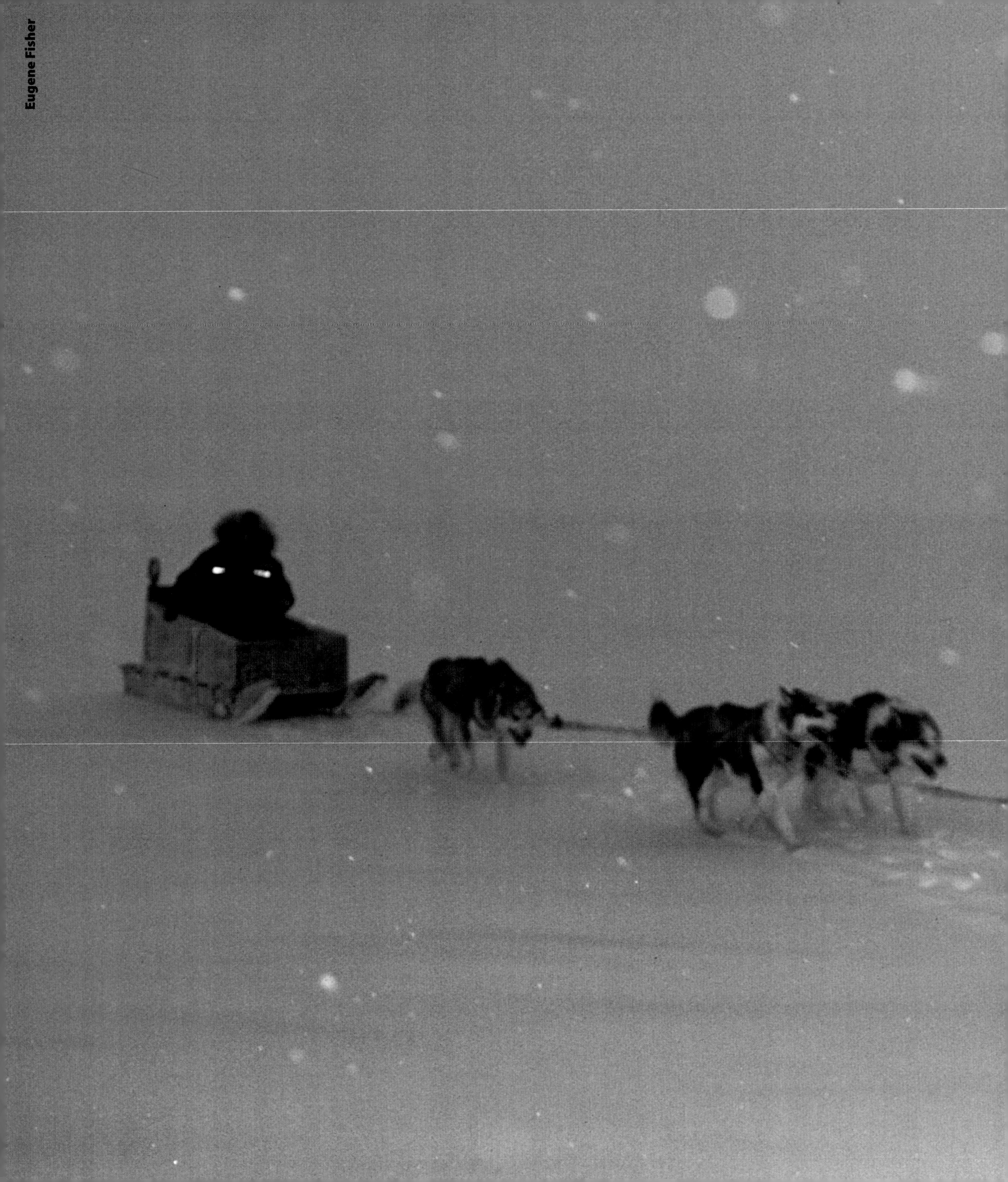

Eugene Fisher

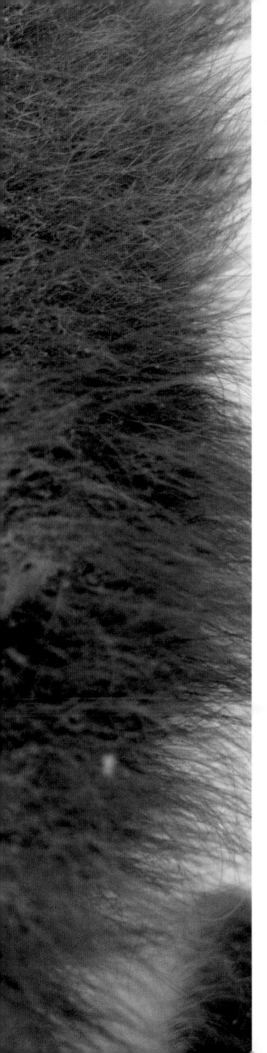

◀ ▲ **Sachs Harbor, Canada**

This Inuit boy has one foot in the Stone Age and the other in cyberspace. His mornings are spent on his father's dogsled traveling across the tundra, cutting ice blocks for water (preceding pages) and hunting caribou for dinner. Afternoons find him surfing the Internet or sending digital pictures of his life to other children around the world. Although for many cultures the collision between old and new can be disastrous, the Inuit hope that they can use technology to weave a tighter web between their far-flung community and the rest of the world. One project involves the debate surrounding ancestral lands. In 1999 the Inuit will gain control of Nunavut, their name for the 600,000 square miles north and west of Hudson Bay. Worried that middlemen may try to profit from tourism on Nunavut, the Inuit plan to use the Net themselves to promote the area and their native crafts. For now, the Inuit are still exploring the technology, which was brought to them on February 8 by Rick Selleck of Systems Engineering Society in Cape Cod, Massachusetts. But with many of the children already feeling comfortable in cyberspace, the Inuits' dream to build worldwide awareness of their rich heritage may soon become a reality.

Photographs by Eugene Fisher

△ **Westfield, England**
▷ **Bradford, England**

Basking in an otherworldly glow, Robert Simpson tours the galaxies. With a click of the mouse, this 15-year-old can touch the stars via a remote link to the Bradford Robotic Telescope. The first robotic telescope wired to the Web, it provides a cosmic eye for astronomers in 72 countries. Requests for a picture of a specific part of the galaxy are sent by email, and only when viewing conditions are optimal does the telescope emerge from the observatory roof to fulfill its tasks. Simpson, who learned about the telescope in school, describes his first foray: "The computer asked me if I wanted to place a job order, and I said yes. Then the screen asked me which galaxy I wanted to see and from what angle. I was like, 'Wow.'" A few days later, Simpson received a photograph of Andromeda to download and share with friends.
Above photograph by Dod Miller
Right photograph by Dario Mitidieri

▲ **Bradford, England**
▷ **Moscow, Russia**

Researching little-known comets, says Russian astronomer Alexander Militsky, is like looking for a pebble in the ocean.
Militsky's work involves complicated calculations and new search technology that explains changes in comet orbits. Painstaking and frustrating though it may be, Militsky's work would be impossible without his Internet link to the Bradford telescope. "There are many astronomers in Russia, but only three or four telescopes," says Militsky. "The best are located in the Asian republics, but because of our political situation, they are closed to me now." Thanks to the Bradford telescope, the vast cosmic ocean is now just a click away.
Above photograph by Dario Mitidieri
Right photograph by Jeremy Nicholl

◀ ▲ **San Diego, California, USA**

In the Global Schoolhouse, kids around the world get a virtual peek at life and learning outside their hometowns. Using words, pictures, video, and audio, students in more than 25 countries come together in this online project to learn about each other's communities. Sparked by the schoolhouse project, students at Martin Luther Middle School in Oceanside created a website for a wild animal park at the nearby San Diego Zoo. Knowing that their words and pictures would be broadcast throughout cyberspace, the students took extra pride in their work. "When they know someone else besides their teacher will be looking at their work, it's a whole different thing," says Barbara Tice-Simons, a teacher at the school. "They recognize that they have a voice in the community—and that inspires them."

Photographs by Rick Rickman

▲ **Atlanta, Georgia, USA**
▶ **Beijing, China**

American students try the penguin shuffle (above). Meanwhile, a student in Beijing makes a papier-mâché version of the bird (right).
Above photograph by Michael A. Schwarz
Right photograph by Adrian Bradshaw

"I'm an explorer, an archeologist, a scientist, a meteorologist, an analyst, a teacher, and a student when I use the Net," says Eric Ebner, a senior at Perham High School in rural Minnesota. Though it may sound a bit grandiose, Ebner's enthusiasm is genuine. As a "research participant" in the Blue Ice: Focus on Antarctica online curriculum, Ebner is one of 9,000 students scattered around the globe who regularly communicate with Dr. Bill Fraser, a scientist studying penguin ecosystems at Palmer Station, Antarctica. On February 8, 1996, third-grade students in Mr. Wright's class at Columbus Avenue School in Valhalla, New York, prepared graphs on the declining krill population, based on data supplied by Dr. Fraser. Meanwhile, students from other schools emailed Fraser their questions: "Why aren't there penguins at the North Pole?" "Have you ever been on an iceberg when it came apart?" Fraser, holed up in a blizzard, patiently answered them all.

◀ ▲ **Grotta degli Scogli Neri, Italy**

Almost every weekend, otherwise normal people crawl through mud, squeeze between rocks, and descend sheer cliffs into absolute darkness beneath the earth's surface. In the world of light, these amateur spelunkers are journalists, doctors, engineers, and students. They're also Web surfers who have turned the Net into a mine of safety information for cave explorers up and down the Italian peninsula. After every descent, members of the Italian Speleological Society post notes and findings on their home page. The result is an instant "living map" of discoveries, hazards, and conditions in caves throughout the country. Not long ago, this sort of knowledge was based on hearsay or local lore. Now, with reliable information available in cyberspace, these explorers can more confidently journey beneath the earth.

Photographs by Enrico Bossan

Manaus, Brazil

The Amazon rain forest may be shrinking, but news of its demise keeps growing on the Net. Constant downloads of data from Brazil's National Institute of Amazonian Research give scientists and environmentalists around the world access to research conducted by and for the organization. The institute, located on a swath of rain forest along the banks of the Amazon River, boasts the only Internet node in the region. On its website, research data collected by resident and visiting scientists is posted along with maps of the area created with global positioning system (GPS) technology. As a result, the Institute's website is fast becoming the world's most vital and comprehensive repository of knowledge about rain forests and the many unique species that inhabit them.
Photographs by Claus C. Meyer

▲ **Angangueo, Mexico**

It's hard to believe that something as ephemeral as a butterfly can make a 2,500-mile journey. And when these delicate creatures alight, they seem to come out of nowhere. But, in fact, every year monarch butterflies make an arduous pilgrimage, beginning in the mountains west of Mexico City and fluttering up the coast as far as Canada. Since 1994, Journey North, an interactive education program, has enabled 25,000 students to use email and the Internet to track the monarch's annual migration. Students along the migratory path post sightings, study conservation, explore geography, and work with real-life applications of math and science related to the monarchs and their journey. Similar Journey North programs cover grizzlies in Yellowstone, caribou near Hudson Bay, humpback whales, peregrine falcons, and leatherback sea turtles.
Photograph by Peter Stone

▶ **Kenyir Lake, Malaysia**

Abang Ramadan, a three-and-a-half-ton rogue Malaysian elephant, was creating nightly havoc in banana plantations. Farmers were up in arms about his midnight snacking habit and the resulting flattened crops. But rather than destroying the hungry creature, on February 8, wildlife rangers tranquilized him, transported him to a national park upriver, and attached a radio collar around his neck. Several times a day, his position is transmitted from the collar via satellite to computers that plot his movements; this information is then charted and posted on the Web. Rangers aren't the only ones keeping a close eye on Abang Ramadan. Along with scientists at the Smithsonian Institute in Washington, D.C., Web surfers also can check in on his wanderings. This ingenious high-tech jungle solution has left everyone happy: The farmers' crops are protected, scientists and naturalists get instantaneous data about wild elephants, and Abang Ramadan dines in peace.
Photographs by David Loh

▷ Fitting a radio collar around the neck of an elephant requires the work and courage of many, but the effort has proved worthwhile. The data transmitted from the collar is posted on the Web, where it has helped wildlife researchers worldwide.

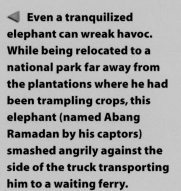

◁ Even a tranquilized elephant can wreak havoc. While being relocated to a national park far away from the plantations where he had been trampling crops, this elephant (named Abang Ramadan by his captors) smashed angrily against the side of the truck transporting him to a waiting ferry.

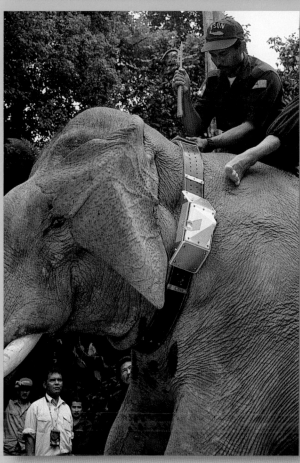

▷ Once the sedation wears off and the chains are removed, the collared elephant will wander away in search of new stomping grounds, none the worse for the journey. As Abang Ramadan wades through the dense forest, satellites and radio transmissions will chart his progress.

David Loh

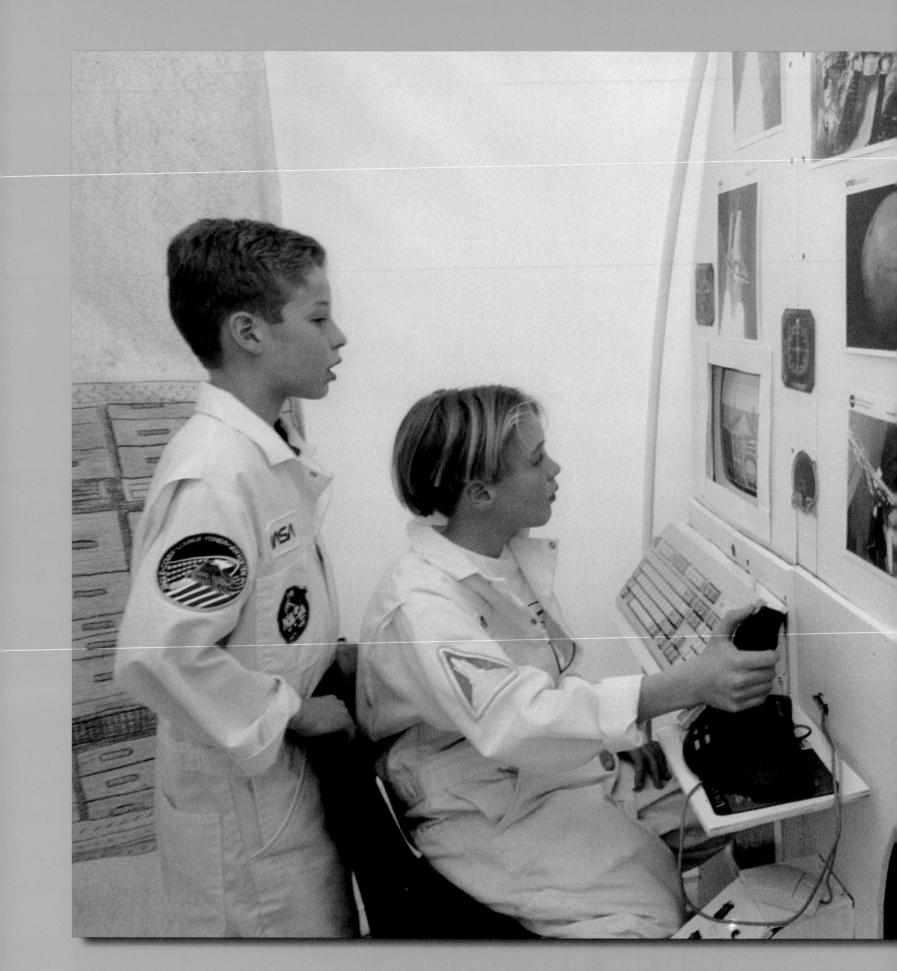

How do you prepare for a journey to Mars? Everyone on this global student team, where ages ranged from seven to 17, had a different answer: In Siberia, students made plans for contact with extraterrestrials. In Argentina, they readied a computer-controlled greenhouse for food supplies. Young British explorers prepared water and soil tests, and American students built command modules. At 00:01 Greenwich mean time on February 8, the yearlong journey began, the most ambitious such space-simulation project to date.

△ **Cleveland, Ohio, USA**

Space mates in Ohio log on from their own simu-lated shuttle.
Photograph by Beth Keiser

◁ **Brownsville, Texas, USA**

At "Mission Control," a kid-constructed command module in Texas, students use CU-SeeMe videoconferencing software.
Photograph by Brad Doherty

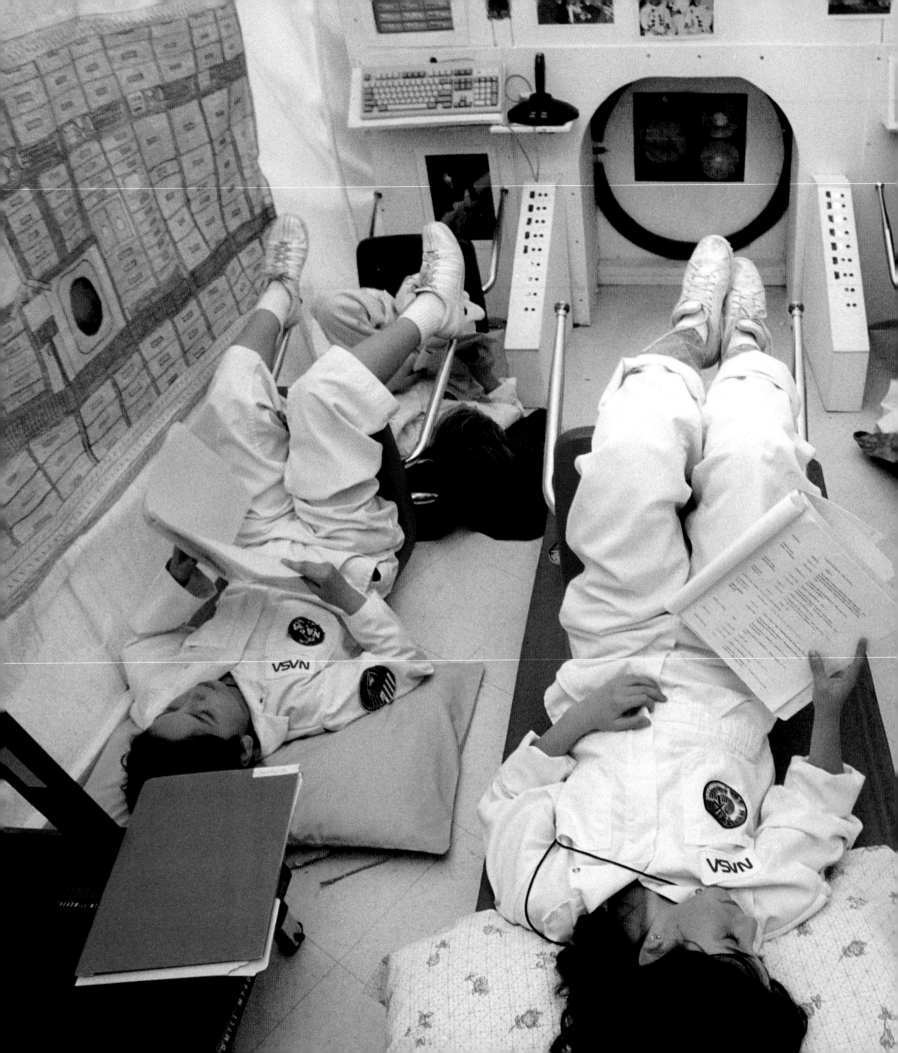

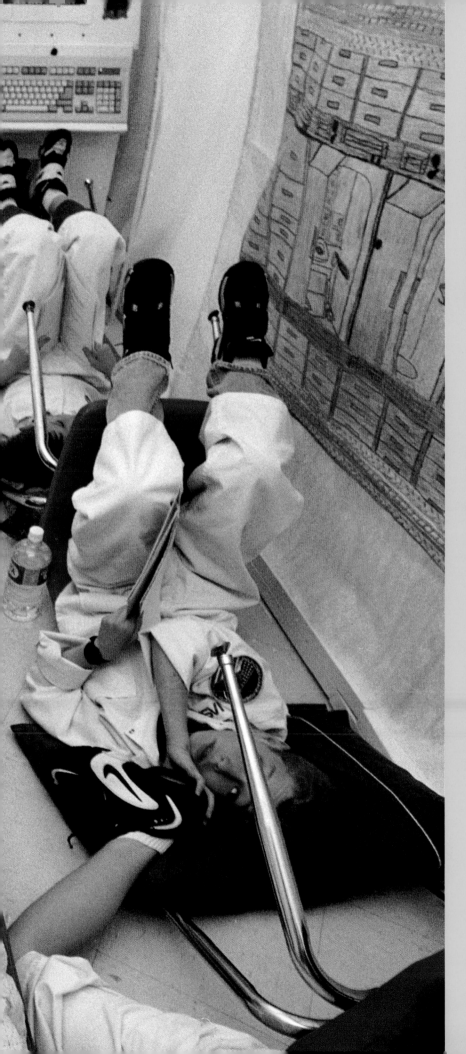

▲ Buenos Aires, Argentina

In Buenos Aires, students get updates on the February 8 launch. *Photograph by Pablo Cabado*

◀ **Brownsville, Texas, USA**

The brainchild of Robert Morgan, a science teacher in Ohio, the Journey to Mars project has captured the imagination of students worldwide. There are formidable technical resources—including shuttle launch-and-docking programs based on NASA software, and tapes of actual flight logs, which were used to develop a working script for the would-be astronauts. But creativity is the real key to this virtual voyage. Here, tipped-back cafeteria chairs simulate the sensation of blastoff, with pillows from home softening the ride. *Photograph by Brad Doherty*

▶ **Exeter, England**

In England, students survey the "Martian" landscape at a local red-sand quarry and collect water samples from the nearby English Channel. *Photograph by David Modell*

◁ **On a chilly Siberian day, students from the Cosmonautic School use a match to launch a rocket on a mock journey to Mars.**

▷ **Zelenogorsk, Siberia**

Ready, set . . . Blastoff! From Siberia, students launch rockets to Mars. In real life, they'll never actually get there, but the learning behind this launch is very real. Students at the Cosmonautic School plotted trajectories for each rocket, using astronomical maps and telescopes. Results were sent via the Net to colleagues around the world, delighting teachers as well as students. "It's incredible that my students get to communicate with kids their age in Siberia," says teacher Chris Rowan of Brownsville, Texas. The fascination is mutual: At the Cosmonautic School, the hallways are lined with email messages from America.
Photography by Nikolai Ignatiev

◁ **With the fuse lit and the rocket ready for takeoff, students run for cover.**

◁ **Their eyes turned skyward, students watch their rocket take off into a gray sky. Results of the launch, the culmination of weeks of study, will be emailed back to "Mission Control" in the United States.**

Sex, Lies, and Websites

There are no limits to the unusual and startling human interactions that are sparked by cyberspace. Weird stuff thrives online because it is a medium affording intimacy on demand, anonymously if one wishes, and without the risk of uninvited physical interaction. It is thus easier for many to be brave and spontaneous online than in person. It is also temptingly easy to reinvent oneself into a cyberpersona quite unrecognizable to friends and family. The "25-year-old co-ed" typing sweet nothings onto your screen is more likely a pimple-faced teenager or a Net-surfing retiree. This sounds like lies, but in the myth-swirl of cyberspace, it can also be art.

While some exploit cyberspace's plasticity and become digital cross-dressers, others opt for the hyperreal. Online diaries are a genre in the making: They have become the creative venue for a new generation of essayists meditating on life's daily minutiae. And words aren't their only tools. Visit Steve Mann's home page and see the world through his "helmetcam," an act of video self-exposure conducted as a symbolic protest against the loss of privacy in modern life.

Meanwhile, cyberspace's intimacy-on-demand is also insinuating itself into our physical spaces. Order a latte and a joint in one Dutch cafe and settle in for some serious Net surfing. The stranger you meet between tokes may just be scarfing a cone in an ice-cream parlor in Bangkok or soaking in a California "geekhaus" hot tub.

You might even find your true love through an email-order-bride service, or simply through an innocent email exchange. This sounds weird to the nonwired, but recall that barely a century ago, romantic telephone chats appalled a generation accustomed to doing such things in person and by letter. Oh, but if you discover that your online romance spills over into the physical world, be sure to describe who you *really* are before you meet.—P.S.

Countries
represented:
Brazil
Canada
Egypt
The Netherlands
Russia
Thailand
USA

▶ **Mountain View, California, USA**

Raven-haired voluptuary and philosopher Romana Machado (left) sells soft-core shots of herself and her friends on the Web—and loves it.
A self-described "software engineer, author, model, and hot-blooded capitalist," Machado sees her work as "erotica without guilt." At her Peek of the Week website, viewers pay via credit card to see shots of this "glamazon" taken by her photographer-husband. "There's no middleman," she says of her small-business venture. "I control the images and reap the benefits." In addition to the pictures, Machado's site includes essays on her beliefs in extropy, a philosophy that includes free markets, smart drugs, and eternal life via cryogenics—freezing your body after death.
Photograph by Jim Gensheimer

"I am going to write whatever I think, whatever happens to me, and let the world be my judge."

—Bryon Sutherland, online diarist

▲ **Denton, Texas, USA**

"I got the impression that something was going on in Lisa's mind last night. Things don't seem quite normal. I was planning on telling her how much she meant to me."

—*The Semi-Existence of Bryon, November 24, 1995*

Photograph by Shelly Katz

▲ **Overland Park, Kansas, USA**

"This morning Bob came downstairs and found me curled up on the dining room floor, surrounded by little snippets of magnetic words. He said, 'What are you doing?' And I said, 'Barb sent me a Shakespearean insult kit—thou monkey-faced, carp-eyed bag of toad puke.' He said, 'Okay, then why are you on the floor?' And I said, 'Well, thou insolent, dog-headed clotpoll (clotpoll?), I spilled them, so I got down on the floor and stayed there.' Yes, I like this."—*Willa's Diary by Willa Cline, 42, legal assistant and online diarist*
Photograph by John Sleezer

Most diarists prefer to keep their private musings under lock and key, but online diaries have spawned a new genre for instant—and intimate—publishing. The electronic journal keepers, whose innermost thoughts are instantly accessible via the Web, are far from homogeneous. Spanning the generations and the issues that surround their particular era, these unlikely authors share everything from didactic prose exploring the meaning of life to well-honed descriptions of everyday life.

"It's thrilling to be so public. Like I said, no secrets."
—*Carolyn Burke*

◀ **Toronto, Canada**

"So I sit here really, honestly wondering about this life thing going on and on. Maybe there is an extrinsic point, maybe I only generate arbitrary intrinsic points, but really . . . it simply continues. And the funny thing is, I'm not sure which way to play it."
—*Carolyn's Diary*
Photograph by Joe Traver

Carolyn Burke, author of Carolyn's Diary, began publishing her thoughts on the Web in January 1995. Since then, her "cognitive landscapes," as she calls her online entries, have won several awards as one of the most interesting sites on the Web. The 30-year-old partner in an Internet consulting firm says she does her best thinking in the bathroom, day or night, whether in a dress or in a tubful of bubbles.

► Cambridge,
Massachusetts,
USA

Steve Mann's
wireless webcam
records his life as
it happens. Steve's
real-time video
can be viewed on
his website, where
he also speaks out
against surveillance
cameras and the
lack of privacy in
modern life.
*Photograph by
Bill Greene*

▲ New York, New York, USA

"It's a lot better than your average phone sex," says a founder of NetMate, the cybersex service that lets clients direct their own online fantasies via typed commands to NetMate entertainers in a New York studio. *Photograph by Andy Levin*

Voyeurism takes on a whole new meaning on the World Wide Web. For MIT graduate student Steve Mann, his omnipresent webcam gear allows him to record life around him. Mann's video view of the world appears instantly on his website and serves as his protest against hidden surveillance cameras, which he says take a "bite out of our souls." At NetMate (right), an online sex service, users don't just watch; they can direct the action. For $4.95 a minute, clients can type in commands, such as "Come closer to the camera" or "Give me a big pout," as NetMate entertainers make cyberfantasies come true.

▲ **Santa Cruz, California, USA**

" 'To geek' is to sit online and read mail, news, chat, and otherwise waste time in front of a keyboard. This 'geeking' often consumes many hours, even if the intention was to 'just log on and check my mail.' Some would say this time would be better spent being social in person or even just being curled up in a sunbeam."—*From the Darkwater website* **Photograph by Mark Richards**

San Francisco, California, USA

Party night at Cyborganic, a virtual home and real-time hangout for cyberartists and pixel-minded folk in San Francisco. *Photograph by William Mercer McLeod*

Boston, Massachusetts, USA

Computer professionals by day, "L0phters" by night, these hackers dumpster-dive for hardware, which they then rebuild into working security networks back at the "L0pht." *Photograph by Bill Greene*

Tucked away in unassuming neighborhoods around the country, geekhauses— a wired version of a kids' clubhouse —are where Netheads indulge their addiction to the digital life. At Darkwater, a longtime geekhaus in Santa Cruz, California, residents go by their Internet identities, such as Omni or Amaroq. When they're not online, Darkwater residents splash, and sometimes Web surf, in the house hot tub (water temperature is controlled remotely via house computers). Like most geekhauses, this one has its own website, a server in the living room and Ethernet ports in each bedroom. With more phone lines than people, this house hums with a cyberspace ambiance that puts it midway between virtual and real.

▲ Portland, Oregon, USA

"We're not your typical computer geeks," says Paisley Lick, 26-year-old mother, herbalist, Web surfer—and professional exotic dancer. As wired entrepreneurs who now use the Web for promotional purposes, Paisley and Deva Lick, her performance partner, have been able to cut down on FedEx bills and broaden their audience by uploading photos for fans and hosting online forums. According to Paisley, the Lick Sisters' website has given them more control over their future and their finances. "With the Web, we're our own marketers," says Paisley. "We decide the image we want to present. The opportunities are endless on the Net—and I really believe those opportunities are there for everybody, no matter who they are, no matter what they do."

Photographs by David Falconer

▶ **Stepping out of their street clothes and into, well, not much at all, the Lick Sisters prepare to go on stage. News of their upcoming performances is posted on the Lick Sisters' website.**

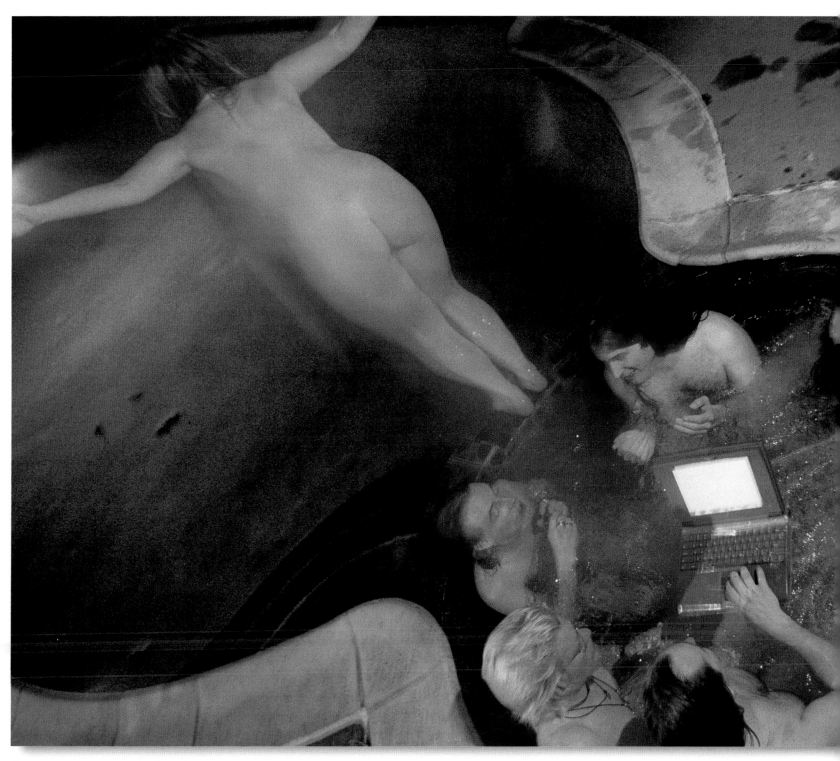

▲ **Santa Cruz, California, USA**

" 'To geek' is to sit online and read mail, news, chat, and otherwise waste time in front of a keyboard. This 'geeking' often consumes many hours, even if the intention was to 'just log on and check my mail.' Some would say this time would be better spent being social in person or even just being curled up in a sunbeam."—*From the Darkwater website* **Photograph by Mark Richards**

▲ New York, New
York, USA

"It's a lot better than your average phone sex," says a founder of NetMate, the cybersex service that lets clients direct their own online fantasies via typed commands to NetMate entertainers in a New York studio. *Photograph by Andy Levin*

Voyeurism takes on a whole new meaning on the World Wide Web. For MIT graduate student Steve Mann, his omnipresent webcam gear allows him to record life around him. Mann's video view of the world appears instantly on his website and serves as his protest against hidden surveillance cameras, which he says take a "bite out of our souls." At NetMate (right), an online sex service, users don't just watch; they can direct the action. For $4.95 a minute, clients can type in commands, such as "Come closer to the camera" or "Give me a big pout," as NetMate entertainers make cyberfantasies come true.

▲ **Portland, Oregon, USA**

"We're not your typical computer geeks," says Paisley Lick, 26-year-old mother, herbalist, Web surfer—and professional exotic dancer. As wired entrepreneurs who now use the Web for promotional purposes, Paisley and Deva Lick, her performance partner, have been able to cut down on FedEx bills and broaden their audience by uploading photos for fans and hosting online forums. According to Paisley, the Lick Sisters' website has given them more control over their future and their finances. "With the Web, we're our own marketers," says Paisley. "We decide the image we want to present. The opportunities are endless on the Net—and I really believe those opportunities are there for everybody, no matter who they are, no matter what they do."

Photographs by David Falconer

▶ **Stepping out of their street clothes and into, well, not much at all, the Lick Sisters prepare to go on stage. News of their upcoming performances is posted on the Lick Sisters' website.**

San Francisco,
California, USA

**Party night at
Cyborganic, a
virtual home and
real-time hangout
for cyberartists
and pixel-minded
folk in San
Francisco.**
*Photograph by
William Mercer
McLeod*

Boston,
Massachusetts,
USA

**Computer profes-
sionals by day,
"L0phters" by
night, these hackers
dumpster-dive for
hardware, which
they then rebuild
into working
security networks
back at the "L0pht."**
*Photograph by
Bill Greene*

**Tucked away in unassuming neighbor-
hoods around the country, geekhauses—
a wired version of a kids' clubhouse —are
where Netheads indulge their addiction to
the digital life.** At Darkwater, a longtime
geekhaus in Santa Cruz, California, residents
go by their Internet identities, such as Omni
or Amaroq. When they're not online,
Darkwater residents splash, and sometimes
Web surf, in the house hot tub (water
temperature is controlled remotely via house
computers). Like most geekhauses, this one
has its own website, a server in the living
room and Ethernet ports in each bedroom.
With more phone lines than people, this
house hums with a cyberspace ambiance that
puts it midway between virtual and real.

Hollywood, California, USA

On TV's "Home Court," actress Pamela Reed plays a judge whose Net-savvy son (Robert Gorman) commits the occasional Internet misdemeanor—such as mistakenly ordering up a prostitute during an innocent email exchange.
Photograph by Dana Fineman

◀ Vancouver, Canada

Creator/executive producer Chris Carter emerges from an alien space vehicle on the set of "The X-Files," whose website gets up to 40,000 hits a day.
Photograph by Ward Perrin

The play's the thing, Shakespeare once said, and he might have added: wherever you find it. These days, ideas flow from one silver screen to another—from the Internet to Hollywood, and back again.

Elyse Singer produced *Love in the Void*, an off-Broadway performance piece based on the tormented online missives of rock diva Courtney Love. Singer also visited an online chat group of Love's fans. There, she found that the anonymity of the Net made for great drama. "They can be quite dramatic because their identity is hidden," says Singer. "They create characters and play roles just like in a theater space, but their stage is cyberspace." In other mediums, of course, the message is different: The TV sitcom "Home Court" portrays the Net as just another part of everyday life, whereas "The X-Files," a popular sci-fi series that has achieved cult status among viewers, encourages fans to critique it online. "We don't have to wait for fan mail. Our America Online forums and official website let us know immediately what our hard-core fans think," says creator/ executive producer Chris Carter. "The Internet has revolutionized television producing."

 New York, New York, USA

Actress Carolyn Baeumler strikes a pose on the set of the off-Broadway production of *Love in the Void*. *Photograph by Joe McNally*

▲ Homewood,
California, USA

**Actress Sharon
Walsh (as Sirena
Vixen) vamps it up
in Ski Vixens from
the X-Dimension,
an online drama
that is part myth,
part B-musical,
and part science
fiction.**
*Photograph by
Olivier Laude*

**They lie, they cheat, they steal, they love,
they live with intrigue—all day and all
night—online.** Free of the constraints of
scheduled programming, some of the Web's
hottest episodic cybersoaps serve up spicy
fare around the clock for wired fans
everywhere. At sites such as The Spot, Web
surfers can send email, eavesdrop on
characters' private thoughts, and scroll
through journal pages that give the inside
story. Interactive features enable fans to
become part of the story, whether it's
choosing a possible outcome, downloading
video of the characters in action, or clicking
on a favorite character to get his or her side of
the story. So far, The Spot is averaging
150,000 hits per day. With costs for producing
a year's worth of cybersoap material roughly
equaling the cost of a single prime-time TV
episode, the Web is destined to become the
next proving ground for up-and-coming
actors and directors anxious to make a debut.

◄ Marina del Rey,
California, USA

**"Spotmates" mourn
the mysterious
disappearance of
their friend, Tara.
Will a body be
found?**
*Photograph by
Aaron Chang*

▶ **Rio de Janeiro, Brazil**

Proving that truth is stranger than fiction, Mìriam Stanescon—a self-proclaimed Gypsy princess—is the inspiration for Brazil's hottest *telenovela.* Each week, some 50 million viewers tune in to "Explode Coraçáo!" ("Explode, Heart!") to watch a Gypsy, based on Stanescon, and the business-man with whom she strikes up an affair over the Internet. The show's writer says her goal was to create a steamy story and show how the Internet embraces "weird and different" people. Stanescon, however, is not amused: She frets that her (television) character lost her virginity before marriage. In court papers, Stanescon claims this amounts to nothing less than defamation of character— her character. Where will it all end? Tune in and find out.
Photograph by Ricardo Azoury

▲ **Amsterdam, The Netherlands**

Today's cybercafes take menu browsing to a whole new level. Offering everything from pixels to pastry, these wired establishments prove that Web surfing does not have to be a solitary activity. For surfers who really want to smoke, there's the Internet Cafe in Amsterdam, a legal "smoke house" where patrons can launch into cyberspace with or without the help of hashish, a cafe specialty. Says Patrick Westborg, 32, who has run the establishment for the past eight years, "It's the best move I ever made. Selling hash is not our main concern anymore. Yes, it's available, but you can just come here for a coffee, or to just surf the Net. The choice is up to you."
Photograph by Arnaud de Wildenberg

▶ Cambridge, Massachusetts, USA

Just off Harvard Square, Cybersmith is the first of a planned international cybercafe chain. The cafe contains 55 computer work-stations, where dining digarati can scan the menu online, play virtual-reality games, or explore the Internet.
Photograph by Stan Grossfeld

▶ Bangkok, Thailand

**For the price of an ice cream cone, Netheads can feed their addiction at Haagen-Dazs. "It's one of the only places in Thailand where people can use the Net for nearly free,"
says one patron.**
Photograph by Peter Charlesworth

▶ Cairo, Egypt

At Fishawi's, one of Cairo's older coffeehouses, poet/writer Ali Darwish discusses the Internet with newspaper reporters and coffeehouse regulars.
Photograph by Barry Iverson

▲ **St. Petersburg, Russia**

Flowers are selected on behalf of an American admirer hoping to win the favor of a prospective Russian bride, whom he selected online.

Photograph by Bill Swersey

▲ **St. Petersburg, Russia**

Natasha posted her picture on the Web with the Shade Introduction Agency. Her electronic efforts paid off with a bouquet of roses from an admirer who first saw her online.
Photograph by Bill Swersey

Red roses, Russia, and email brides weave a web of romance on the Internet. Now lonely singles from around the world don't have to frequent the usual haunts, such as bars or church groups, to find a mate. Shade, an agency in St. Petersburg, Russia, posts pictures of available women on the Web. With a click of the mouse and a credit-card fee of $19.95, interested parties can have a Shade representative deliver a token of their affection (roses are the preferred gesture) to the lucky woman. As is the case with most romances—wired or otherwise—things can get more complicated after that, but Shade founder Kirill Klimov says suitors are more than willing to overcome any obstacles that stand between them and their long-distance loves. "There's a market out there," he says. "I often receive more than 20 email messages a week from romance seekers around the world."

▷ **Holmen, Wisconsin, USA**

"When I saw the scanned image of Anna, my heart skipped a beat. I immediately scanned my own photo and sent it. Emails ensued . . . "Jim Pratt, email lover and now husband of Anna Nasova, his Russian bride and mother of their child, Deanna.
Photograph by Ron Johnson

The cyberlove story of Mark Robbins and Leslie Salzmann had the usual ups and downs of any '90s courtship. They first noticed each other in a BBS chat room. When Robbins took a peek at Salzmann's bio and saw many of the characteristics he had hoped for in a mate, he asked her out. Thinking he was yet another chat-room creep, Salzmann ignored him. A month later she came around, and the two met for a quick lunch that ended up lasting seven hours. Thousands of emails later, despite jobs in two different cities, the two married. Salzmann wanted to wed in cyberspace, but Robbins put his foot down. "I thought it would be cool to marry using a CU-SeeMe site, but Mark wanted to be able to hold my hand at the wedding," says Salzmann. *Photograph by Olivier Laude*

◀ **Winter Park, Florida, USA**

Tracy Borders (previous page), a single mother of seven, credits America Online and pen-pal Buz Schuler with helping her rebuild her life. She moved from Hawaii to Florida to meet him after exchanging emails for months. Four-year-old Kyle just wishes they'd stop kissing.
Photograph by Bill Frakes

▲ San Francisco, California, USA

True love takes all forms, shapes, and lifestyles. The anonymity and instant access afforded by the Net has enabled some unusual couples to find each other more easily than ever before. Allyn Gallant and Sherilyne Moffitt are connected to each other in a way that other lovers only experience metaphorically. After meeting in a newsgroup for enthusiasts of sadomasochism, an alternative lifestyle that involves chains, leashes, and whips, they quickly decided to become "bonded" for life. Says Gallant, "We have many interests in common, not the least of which are our shared sexual practices. She has signed a contract to be my slave for life. I love her and she loves me."
Photograph by Acey Harper

"After finding and answering an ad on an Internet newsgroup, I met my love. She and I have been together for three months now and plan to stay together for life."
—*Allyn Gallant*

Open for Business

Countries represented:

Germany

India

Japan

Singapore

South Africa

USA

Vietnam

◀ **Carmel, Indiana, USA**

When collector Gene Van Hove traveled from Indiana to New York to find the perfect Rafal Olbinski painting, he didn't expect to find it on a computer. But he did. As part of ArtView, an online service linking participating galleries across the country, the New York art dealer assisting Van Hove was able to hyperlink to a gallery in New Orleans, where his client found the painting of his dreams. Within days, it was sent to him for approval. Van Hove wonders why online galleries are only just now taking off. "This is the future," he says. "It's the best way to shop." *Photograph by Ron Goebel*

The word commerce *was anathema in cyberspace barely three years ago, but now it's the norm as businesses around the world set up shop online. It started with small storefronts selling specialty items, but has grown quickly into a parallel universe: In cyberspace, one can now buy everything from dog ribbons to megabucks art, as well as access bank accounts, trade stocks, job hunt, and even be discovered—a cyberfeat that many budding rock stars have already accomplished.*

This represents nothing less than a shift from physical marketplace to digital marketspace. Moreover, this is a marketspace in which there is no distance between two points. For an artist in Singapore, a world audience seemed only a dream; now, her Web gallery draws global viewers with the click of a mouse. And World Relief in Illinois has discovered that using email to link up with its Vietnamese loan recipients has cut miles of red tape, enabling village women to get ahead by starting small businesses.

This does not mean that the physical "place" of stores, banks, and workplaces will disappear. Rather, it is growing into a larger, more metaphysical "space" made up of both physical location and emerging electronic arenas. Thus, the monks of Holy Cross Abbey can preserve the cherished spiritual solitude of their remote monastery by pursuing work as electronic scriveners in cyberspace.

This emerging marketspace represents a dramatic influx of variety in our global business environment. More players, more markets, more choices, and more flexibility all translate into more business. And, of course, a marketspace open for business is a hotbed of individual entrepreneurship. Joichi Ito, a young Japanese entrepreneur is wiring cafes and clubs in Tokyo's hippest neighborhood. And the founders of PlanetOut, an alternative online service, wheeled and dealed their cybersavvy into a big-bucks venture capital deal.

These examples all show that cyberspace is indeed open for business, but amid all the excitement, the new marketspace has barely begun to reveal its full measure of surprise. Without doubt, the surprises will include more than a few business failures and some wrenching shifts. But this is nothing new, progress is not always built on the spires of earlier technology, it's often built on the ruble.—P.S.

San Carlos, California, USA

On February 8, Greg Miller, president of Tenadar Software, called a staff meeting to review the company's latest business plan. Unlike many harried executives, 11-year-old Miller actually looks forward to these gatherings. "When we have a meeting, we have tons of food and a lot of fun," he says. *Fun* is the operative word at Tenadar. Miller launched the company in 1995 after designing Prince of India, a software game he and his friend distributed on the Net as shareware. After Yahoo picked the game as one of its weekly Cool Links, Miller decided to transform the company from a nonprofit organization to a viable business. With the motto "Great software for kids, by kids," Miller and his staff, ages 10 to 12, post their games on the Tenadar website. The goal, according to Miller, is "to earn a little money and encourage kids to get involved with computers."

Photographs by Doug Menuez

◀ **Eleven-year-old Greg Miller, president of Tenadar Software, calls a staff meeting at his kitchen table. "Miles Davis," the company mascot, waits not so patiently outside.**

◁ Mountain View, California, USA

At 24, Marc Andreessen is the youngest of the Web's founding fathers. His contributions include the Mosaic prototype (the first Web browser) and Netscape Navigator, the browser used by three of every four Web surfers.
Photograph by Doug Menuez

◁ Aspen, Colorado, USA

While a UC-Berkeley student, Bill Joy developed a version of AT&T's UNIX operating system and tailored it for the Internet. Joy is now cofounder and vice president of research for Sun Microsystems.
Photograph by David Hiser

◁ Boston, Massachusetts, USA

Bob Metcalfe helped lay the Web's foundation by inventing Ethernet, the current standard for local area networks. Now a pundit for *Infoworld*, Metcalfe is considered a voice of reason in the technology world.
Photograph by Stan Grossfeld

◁ Cambridge, Massachusetts, USA

Tim Berners-Lee created HyperText Markup Language (HTML), which enables linking graphical onscreen documents to others on the Net. Together with "browser" viewers, HTML documents make up the World Wide Web.
Photograph by Sam Ogden

If the virtual community of cyberspace had a town park, statues of these men would grace its grounds. From the founding father of the Web to the developer of Netscape Navigator, these men are living proof that the creativity and vision of individuals fuel the fire behind the digital revolution. Through their work, the Internet has gone from a cold-war tool to a place where people of all nations can have a voice.

PlanetOut founder
Tom Rielly (right)
power lounges with
Ron Buckmire,
founder of the
Queer Resources
Directory.

◀ Beverly Hills, California, USA

PlanetOut, an online service geared to gays and lesbians, is in the right place at the right time. Statistics indicate that a tremendous number of gay households are online. One reason: The anonymity of cyberspace may be preferable to joining an organization or subscribing to a magazine. Enter PlanetOut. Along with daily news feeds, it features music, movie and book reviews, and a political action center. Investors are confident that PlanetOut will soar. Already, it has $3 million in financing from backers including Sequoia Venture Capital and America Online. "The timing couldn't be better," says founder Tom Rielly. "Everyone is acknowledging the role of 'community' in successful Internet enterprises, and that's exactly what PlanetOut is doing."
Photograph by Dana Fineman

▲ Berlin, Germany

An actor in Berlin begins his lines. Across the globe, a sound technician in California adjusts the bass level for the actor's voice. Seconds later, the audio director replays the tape and calls it a wrap. It's the wonderful world of Disney—in cyberspace. From the same people who made Mickey Mouse an international icon, a new technology enabling foreign-language dubbing in real time is now drastically cutting the time it takes to make Disney's new movies available in more than 29 languages. Disney's Digital Interactive Audio Link (DIAL) transmits audio signals over a special digital network with no audible loss of sound quality. With this virtual sound studio, it truly is a small world after all.
Photograph by Jorg Muller

▲ **Pasadena, California, USA**

In 1993 Perry Lopez and Monica Bosserman Lopez opened a small store to sell their specialty hot sauces and foods. Business was good, but not good enough. Hoping to find a market beyond their community, the couple decided that a website, rather than mail order, was the way to go. Although the site cost $20,000, the Lopezes felt that the long-term savings on postage and printing, and the chance to reach more people, would offset the expense. To their amazement, the payback was quick: More than 1,000 visitors drop by the Hot Hot Hot site daily, and 20 percent of the company's sales come from site visitors. "So many people know about us," says Monica. "People from everywhere come into the store because of the site. It's incredible."

Photograph by Douglas Kirkland

▲ Jeffersontown, Kentucky, USA

Just as a side trip down a blue highway can lead to the perfect slice of apple pie at a local diner, traveling the byways of the information superhighway can lead to some unlikely discoveries. For example, the last thing you might expect while Web surfing is the perfect dog ribbon—but you can find it at Eleanor and Charles Stoess' online pooch-accessory business. The Stoesses started out with dog shampoo but now concentrate on the ribbons, which they offer in an assortment of styles and holiday themes. "We have St. Patrick's day bows with leprechauns and shamrocks; an Easter bow with bunnies and chicks; a July 4th bow—which is, of course, red, white, and blue," notes Eleanor. The Stoesses make and ship 250,000 bows a year, and although the online portion of their business started out slow, they're confident it will pick up. "It's a nice addition to our retirement income," says Eleanor.
Photograph by Bill Luster

▲ **Atlanta, Georgia, USA**

Bassist Allen Whitman of the Mermen uses every spare moment on the road to respond to email from fans and write his weekly column for the group's website.
Photograph by Gary Chapman

The newest route to the top of the charts may be the information superhighway. That's the conclusion of musicians such as The House Jacks, an a cappella group that has linked with fans on its website since 1993. Online enthusiasts can click on the site to read about band members, send them email, check tour dates, view photos, order CDs, and hear song selections from the group's latest work. The Mermen, an instrumental rock group, credits its website with landing them out-of-state gigs. "We got a show in Miami because someone saw our site, picked up our CD, and called a local radio station about it. Next thing you know, the deejay is calling for an interview. One thing just led to another," says Mermen bassist Allen Whitman.

▷ **San Francisco, California, USA**

The House Jacks, a wired a cappella group, reaches out to its audience both in person and online.
Photograph by Ed Kashi

Artist Lin Hsin Hsin has built a cyberspace museum devoted to her work.

Andy Warhol once said that everyone has 15 minutes of fame, but artist Lin Hsin Hsin will always be in the spotlight. Complete with an online gift shop that displays her publications, the Lin Hsin Hsin Art Museum is a one-woman show with no end in sight. Visitors can view videos of Hsin Hsin discussing her work, read the artist's poetry, or wander through galleries featuring her art. While most artists struggle to find opportunities to exhibit their work, Hsin Hsin reaches a worldwide audience with her cyberspace museum. So far, her site, which opened in 1995, has hosted more than 100,000 visitors from 64 countries. Hsin Hsin says that the purpose of the museum is not to make a profit but to provide a place to use the latest technology, educate the public, and encourage art appreciation. Still, the innovative website has boosted her career. "I've been invited to participate in a number of exhibitions and festivals over the Net as a result of my online museum," she says.

Photograph by R. Ian Lloyd

▲ Tokyo, Japan

After years of dominance in electronics, Japan ironically finds itself playing catchup in the Internet world—which it's now doing with a vengeance.

Cellular phones are omnipresent in Japan, but the Internet has had a harder time catching on with the country's gadget elite. One reason may be the high cost of extra phone lines, which can run up to $700 each, making Web surfing from home prohibitively expensive. Enter Joichi "Joi" Ito, a 30-year-old entrepreneur who is wiring the cafes and clubs of Harajuku, Tokyo's hippest neighborhood. According to Ito, technology is just another part of daily life for the Japanese: "Most young women carry pagers, and they have certain number codes that can mean 'I love you' or 'I'm thinking of you,'" he says. Ito believes the leap from pagers to email should be a snap, and the numbers bear him out: At last count, Japan's Internet user base was growing 14 percent per month.
Photograph by Torin Boyd

Joi Ito, Japan's "Mr. Internet," and cyberspace teen idol Reiko Chiba stroll Harajuku, the trendy Tokyo neighborhood that Ito hopes to wire.

New Delhi, India

A unique combination of paperless technology, scraps of real paper, and hard work has turned these village women into the owners of a new handmade paper-making business. At TARA (Technology and Action for Rural Advancement), a division of Development Alternatives, the crude mud walls of the building mask what is the highest-tech communications center for miles. Here, in a poverty-stricken area outside of New Delhi, Development Alternatives staff are building a database to catalog information on sustainable-development projects, such as the paper-making project pictured on these pages. The latest communications technology combines with the ancient art of paper-making in this new venture. As a result, these women are gaining job experience as well as respect from their community. *Photographs by Pablo Bartholomew*

▲ **Combining technology and craftsmanship, the TARA project has created jobs for village women. Here, workers dry sheets of hand-made paper in the sun.**

▷ **Stellenbosch, South Africa**

The Community of Living Water, a development group in an impoverished South African township, has been using the Net at a nearby training center to gather information on adult-literacy programs and farming skills. Nontsikelelo Phalla (pictured in the blue dress on the following page) has passed her third level of Adult Basic Education via the Internet. *Photograph by Louise Gubb*

Hanoi, Vietnam

In a country where mail delivery is highly unreliable, faxes are exorbitant, and corruption is rampant, a small-business loan program went online to change women's futures—$42 at a time. Although it may not seem like much to those in the developed world, the average World Relief loan of $42 in seed money has meant the difference between starting a small business, such as the poultry farm and the beauty salon pictured here, or remaining in poverty. World Relief, an Illinois-based development agency, uses email to bypass the Vietnamese postal system and cut down on fax costs (a one-page fax from Hanoi to the United States can cost as much as $20). So far, the program has distributed more than $300,000 to more than 4,800 Vietnamese women. *Photographs by Lois Raimondo*

Models and editors get ready for a "Geek Chic" fashion shoot at Fashion Internet.

Once the domain of the nerdy, cyberspace is now the hottest venue for the trendy fashion set. In a world where designers rise and fall faster than hemlines, an online magazine may be the best way for real fashion junkies to get up-to-the-minute coverage. At Fashion Internet, an online magazine, visitors can scroll through a designer's entire line or enter a chat room and discuss the latest trends. In addition to breaking news, Fashion Internet recently launched an online casting call for models. Cybersearch winners will be chosen from electronically submitted photos and featured in an online fashion spread.
Photograph by Dustin Pittman

△ **Upper Montclair, New Jersey, USA**

Looking for a quick read? Try the 60-second novelist.
Dan Hurley used to ply his trade on street corners,
pounding out life stories on his Royal manual typewriter
for anyone willing to pay. In 1995 Hurley was discovered
by America Online and relegated his typewriter to the
closet. Now, at Hurley's regular spot in cyberspace,
interested parties can email Hurley their life details, which
he then spins into humorous, 60-second versions. For an
online client named MsDesire, Hurley wrote a fitting little
story: "Once upon a time, a little tigress was released upon
the world. . . . She gave full vent to all her passions and
became the Walt Whitman of desire. . . . " The story went
on, but not for long. MsDesire's reaction was immediate:
"I love you. Thank you," read her email.
Photograph by Misha Erwitt

**Dan Hurley writes
"byte-sized" life
stories online.**

Berryville, Virginia, USA

For centuries, monks have been the keepers of records, the scribes of books. Recently Edward Leonard, an account executive at a computer company, had an epiphany. Realizing that the monks at a nearby abbey were in need of outside income, Leonard came up with the Electronic Scriptorium, a document- and imaging-conversion service for businesses provided by monks. The virtual corporation links 15 monasteries around the country. In 1995 the company earned $1.5 million. At the Holy Cross Abbey, the original recipient of Leonard's technical help, the monks have added a home page where they sell the house specialty: fruitcakes.
Photographs by Nick Kelsh

▷ **Edward Leonard (right) meets with Father Andrew Gries at the Holy Cross Abbey. The abbey is one of 15 around the country that make up the Electronic Scriptorium.**

Aspen, Colorado, USA

It's 2 a.m. on a snowy winter night, and somehow—among the mirrored disco ball, laser lights, and keyboard—taxi driver Jon Barnes manages to find the steering wheel of his multitasking hack. Billed as the Ultimate Taxi, Barnes' cybermobile cruises the streets while passengers surf the Web via a cellular modem. For his next trick, Barnes is working with technical wizard and friend Harvie Branscomb (above) to connect a camera to the laptop computer. "I want to take live pictures of my passengers and send them to my home page," says Barnes. "Imagine watching a live picture of yourself on the Web while you ride the streets of Aspen. I'm billing it as 'The first light-speed ride.' "

Photograph by David Hiser

▲ **New York, New York, USA**

Remember when it was a big deal that Barbie could bend her legs? Not anymore. At R/GA studios, an actress clad in a motion-capture harness acts out Barbie's scripted moves, enabling a digitally animated Barbie to react with lifelike movements. R/GA studios has also created other out-of-this-world film sequences, such as basketball giant Shaquille O'Neal competing against clones of himself in the ultimate game of one-on-one. Robert M. Greenberg, cofounder of R/GA, says that the high-speed networks he uses let artists at different sites create virtual studios. "Online collaboration breaks down the limitations imposed by geography and time," he says.
Photograph by Gregory Heisler

▲ **Alexandria, Virginia, USA**

When two brothers went online as fools with investment advice, 200,000 disciples decided it was no joke.

In 1994 friends and relatives made up the mailing list for Tom and David Gardner's investment newsletter. But since linking up with America Online, the two brothers, known online as The Motley Fool, have added 25 full-time staffers to help deal with their growing business. Their followers know a good thing when they see it: The Gardners' portfolio currently outperforms all major stock indexes, a success they attribute to "doing [our] homework." But according to Erik Rydholm, a partner in The Motley Fool company, the most important ingredient is the interaction with online readers: "More than half our content comes from the investors who make tracking company performances their business. The constant feedback from these people allows us to keep improving what we do."

Photograph by Dirck Halstead

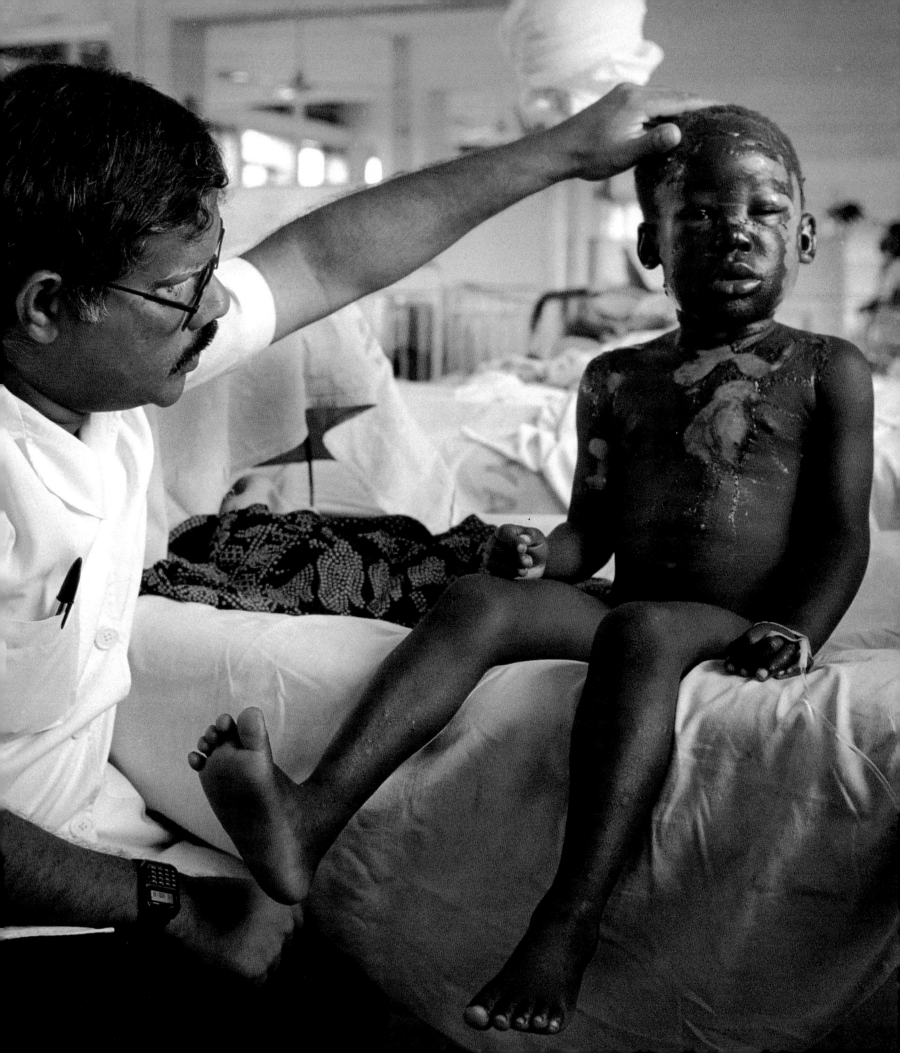

To the Rescue

Countries represented:

Canada

Egypt

Russia

Tanzania

Thailand

USA

Wales

◀ **Dar es Salaam, Tanzania**

Open cooking fires are common in the third world. So are burn injuries among children. In the past, Dr. Primo Carneiro of the Muhimbili Medical Center had to rely on limited supplies to treat his pediatric burn patients. With HealthNet, a satellite-based network for health workers, the doctor now has global resources. HealthNet put Dr. Carneiro in touch with the Health Foundation in New York, which responded with advice, information, and a free shipment of phenytoin, a drug that promotes healing in burn patients. In 1995 HealthNet also allowed physicians in central Africa to share information during the deadly ebola outbreak. *Photograph by Malcolm Linton*

B efore cyberspace came to the rescue, matching organs with recipients was a chancy thing. Coordinators would race the clock, furiously dialing hospitals until the right match was found. More often than not, organs went to waste instead of saving lives. Now matches are made in cyberspace. Even with this electronic donor program, the placement process is still a race against time. But online technology has tilted the odds decisively in favor of hospital and patient.

Similar tales of rescue, large and small, are coming in from all corners of cyberspace. Doctors in Africa consult electronically with burn specialists in U.S. medical centers, working together to save children burned by the open fires common in rural villages. Parents who once coped alone with devastatingly ill children now find comfort and practical advice among a cybercommunity of others facing the same challenges. An elderly shut-in begins to explore the Net, only to discover new friends and companions.

Cyberspace is emerging as a force for community and civility in areas beyond basic health care. Police officers on bicycles are now packing laptops as well as the more traditional tools of law enforcement. The World Wide Web has become home to Most Wanted posters that once adorned post office walls. Air Force personnel who once awaited nuclear Armageddon beneath a granite mountain now use the same technology created for the cold war to track "space garbage" and earthbound asteroids. And the Starbright Foundation has set up a shared multimedia cyberspace in which seriously ill children can interact with each other.

Of course, not all online rescues are without controversy. DeathNet is a resource for sufferers of terminal illnesses seeking a means of self-euthanasia. Although participants are carefully screened, the question remains: Might DeathNet also encourage depressed people to consider suicide? The stories here do not merely inspire but raise deep and troubling issues of morality and ethics as well.

However, cyberspace does not merely come to the rescue, it also makes otherwise invisible acts of rescue visible to the rest of us. In so doing, it invites us to help and to consider consequences, and this could be the most important benefit of all.—P.S.

◀ ▲ Lancaster, Ohio, USA

Her days are spent in darkness; her voice is no more than a whisper. But in her online world, Georgia Griffith sheds light on issues and regularly communicates with 20,000 people around the world. Though blind since birth and deaf for the past 25 years, Griffith hosts seven CompuServe forums covering politics, religion, and current events. Every day from 5 a.m. to 9 p.m., she switches among the five computers that crowd the spare bedroom of her modest home. Griffith was once limited to conversations traced out on her palms; with the help of a braille reader connected to her computers, she now has the world at her fingertips. Most of her online followers aren't even aware of her handicaps, which to her makes the cyberworld more real than her physical life. "It's the people I meet and the opportunities to share with them that makes the online world such a delightful place to spend my time," says Griffith.

Photographs by Beth Keiser

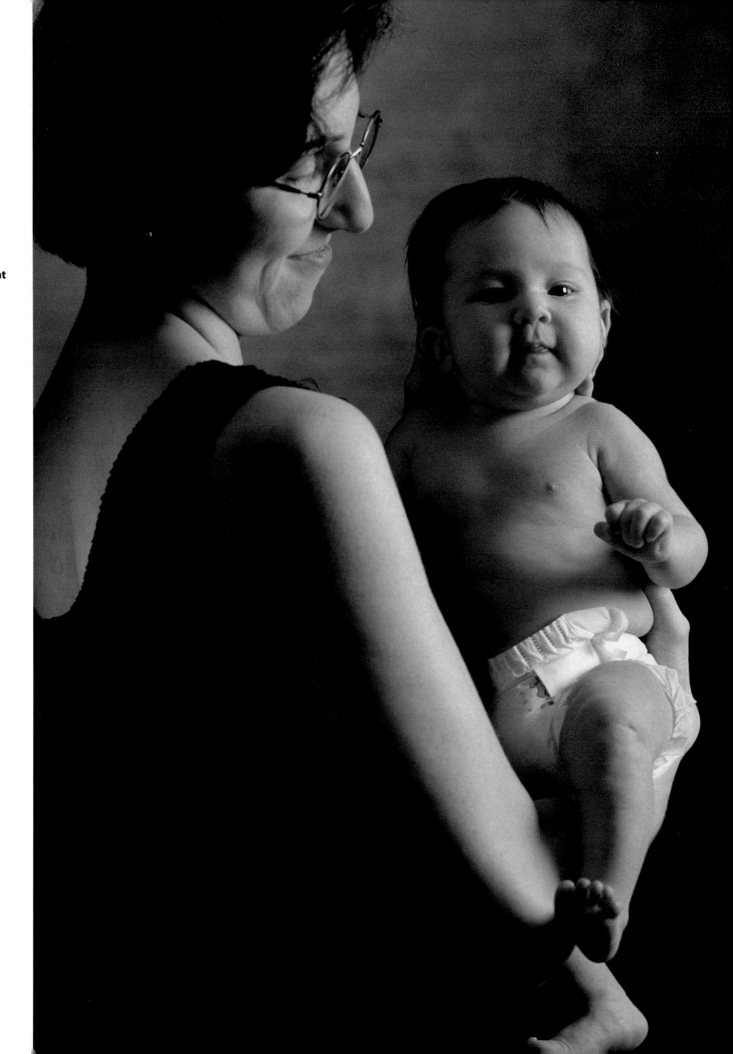

Phaedra Hise went to cyberspace for support during her pregnancy.

▲ Oklahoma City, Oklahoma, USA

As America reeled in the aftermath of the Oklahoma City bombing that killed 167 people in 1995, two Muslim students used the Net to scoop the mainstream media. Even before rescue units were fully deployed, early reports speculated on a link to Islamic terrorists. Worried about a possible backlash against Muslims, Mas'ood Cajee and Mueed Ahmad, University of Oklahoma students and editors/producers of the school's Oklahoma Daily Online newspaper, went into action, posting an article (by students Nicole Koch and Gregory Potts) that suggested the bombing was related to the one-year anniversary of the incineration of a Branch Davidian compound in Waco, Texas. The connection proved correct, and suddenly the Daily Online's website became a major news source, with 20,000 visitors a day following the coverage supplied by 10 student reporters. Editor Gian Trotta of Pathfinder, Time Inc.'s website, said the Daily Online did better than good: "They deserve an electronic Pulitzer for how quickly they got the information up."
Photograph by John Gapps III

◀ Somerville, Massachusetts, USA

With a rare and painful form of arthritis, Phaedra Hise wondered whether she could bear the stress of pregnancy and birth. Hise suffers from ankylosing spondylitis, a condition that left her own father with a spine so stiffened that he couldn't bend over to tie his shoes. Even in a metropolitan area like Boston, Hise couldn't find a support group to answer her questions, and her doctor had only treated a few other patients with the disease. When Hise and her husband wanted to start a family, she was terrified. "I didn't know if I could take medication during a pregnancy," she says, "and I couldn't imagine carrying and delivering a baby with this pain." Through an online arthritis support group, Hise found answers to her questions and the reassurance she needed. On December 13, 1995, Hise posted an important note to her online supporters: "Please welcome Lily Anthea. Mother and baby are fine."
Photograph by Steve Krongard

Pattaya, Thailand

In Thailand, a group of disabled students regularly travel the information super-highway, communicating with other disabled people around the world.

Through their listings on the Flying Wheelchair BBS (bulletin board service), the students at the Redemptorist Vocational School have been amazed to learn of the legislation passed in other countries to aid the disabled. Strange and wonderful concepts such as kneeling buses, mandatory access ramps, and public restrooms designed to accommodate disabled people have motivated some of the students to educate their own communities. Yet, in a country where traffic jams are legendary and the AIDS epidemic rages unchecked, whether the government will prioritize the needs of the disabled remains a real question. None-theless, the students seem far from discouraged. "The Internet makes me feel free of my disability," one student enthused. "On the Net, I don't feel like a handicapped person."
Photograph by Peter Charlesworth

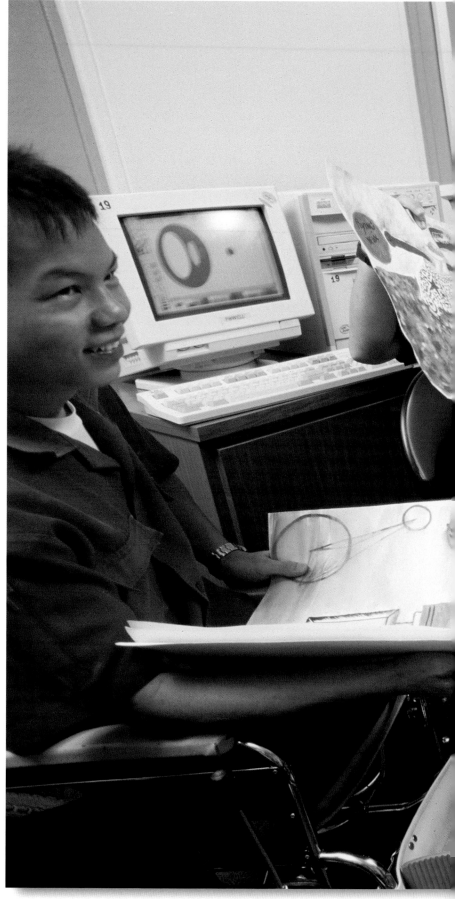

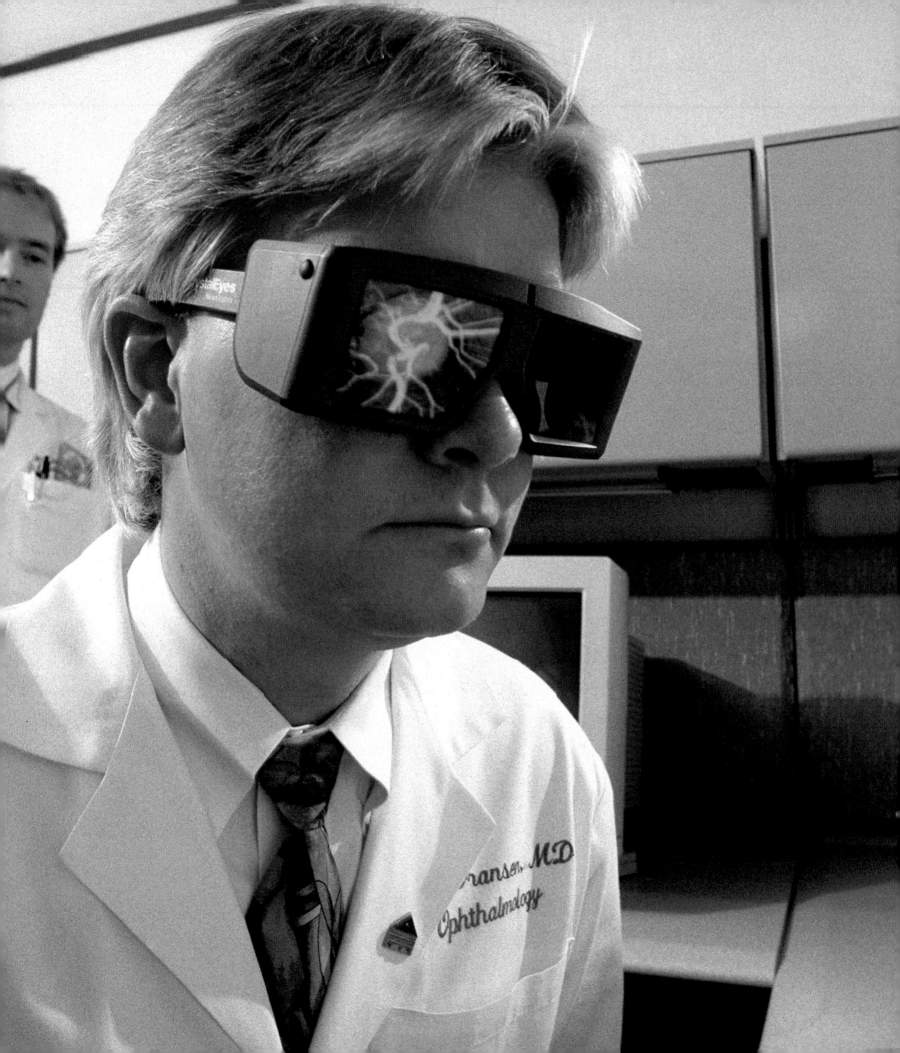

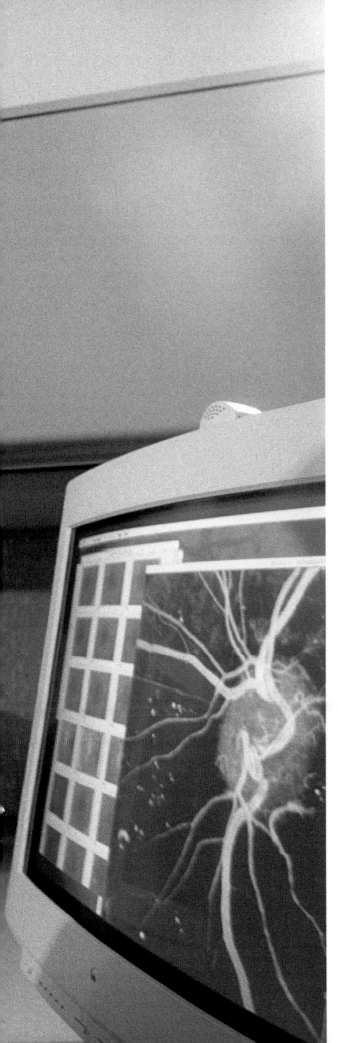

◀ Oklahoma City, Oklahoma, USA

Imagine losing your sight just because the doctor who could have diagnosed the problem was a mere 82 miles away. That was the problem for many Chickasaw Indians in rural Oklahoma. Chickasaws are at genetic risk for diabetic retinopathy, a degenerative disease that results in blindness. The condition is treatable, but the real problem was transporting patients to the Dean McGee Eye Institute in Oklahoma City, 82 miles away. Today, however, digital photography and the Internet are doing the job: Doctors at the Chickasaw's home clinic send digital images via the Net to ophthalmologists at Dean McGee, who don infrared-controlled 3-D glasses to review the retina scans. The result: quick diagnoses and a brighter future for some 7,000 diabetics who are Chickasaws.
Photograph by John Gapps III

▲ Montgomery, Wales

In this small Welsh town, where sheep outnumber people four to one, the same technology used to help Chickasaw Indians (see left) is hard at work. Thanks to Tele-Education and Medicine (TEAM), a project that links doctors in rural Wales with medical experts 150 miles away, townspeople and their doctors are guaranteed instant access to ophthalmologists trained to diagnose diabetic retinopathy. TEAM also provides links to specialists in other fields, such as dermatology, asthma, and physiotherapy. "Patients prefer attending local 'teleconsultations' rather than traveling to hospital clinics," says one TEAM consultant. "Our project brings together doctors and specialists over the electronic examining table."
Photograph by Daniel Meadows

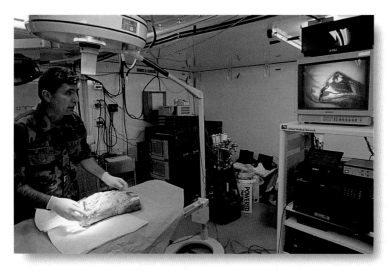

◀ Washington, D.C., USA

The image of a soldier with a bullet wound in his head appeared on the computer screen. Suddenly, the doctors at Walter Reed Army Medical Center fell silent. They'd seen thousands of medical photos before, but this one, of a soldier thousands of miles away in Somalia, will be forever etched in their memories. "There was a real patient with a real injury," says Dr. Edward Gomez, head of telemedicine research and development at Walter Reed. "Until then, our work was theoretical, but suddenly the face of telemedicine, with all its possibilities, unmasked itself." Since then, Dr. Gomez and his team have developed a fully deployable telemedicine unit that can be used to transmit data and digital images to medical experts at Walter Reed from anywhere in the world.
Photograph by Dirck Halstead

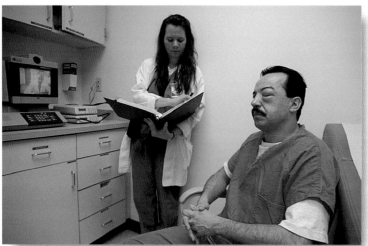

▲ **Englewood, Colorado, USA**

Transferring inmates from the Arapahoe County Detention Facility to doctors in Denver, 20 miles away, was a logistical nightmare. Security was a concern, along with making sure that patients were really sick enough to warrant special treatment outside of jail. But now inmates can receive medical care via cyberlink: Using two-way video-conferencing, doctors in Denver examine prisoners and prescribe treatments. So far, the year-old program, which cost about $20,000 to implement, has saved Arapahoe County about $100,000 in transportation and security costs. Supporters of the program say that it gives prisoners access to far-away specialists who might not otherwise be available. The Denver Department of Health and Hospitals plans to implement the pilot program statewide to serve Colorado's 11,000 inmates.
Photograph by Paul Chesley

▶ **Menlo Park, California, USA**

Someday, cybersurgery may save soldiers' lives on the field of battle. Picture a stretcher equipped with robotic arms that can mimic the hand movements of a surgeon miles away. Though cybersurgery sounds far-fetched, scientists at SRI International are working to create just that. As part of a Pentagon project called Remote Telepresence Surgery, scientists have developed technology enabling doctors to use 3-D images, stereo sound, and force-reflecting manipulators to direct and control on-site robots, which perform surgical procedures. "As the surgeon touches the tissue, he feels the tissue," says SRI's Dr. Ajit Shah. Currently, the project is in the experimental stage, though further advances in wireless communications could extend the reach of a skilled surgeon to patients up to 1,000 miles away.
Photograph by Kim Komenich

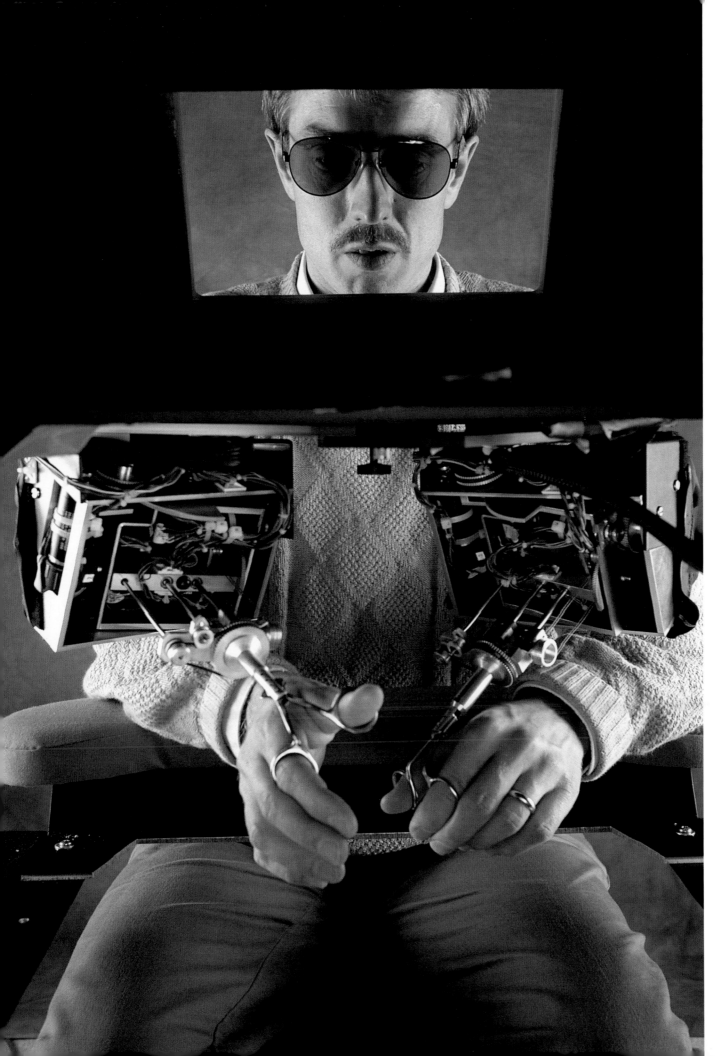

Enclosed in SRI's remote-surgery console, a doctor uses wired manipulators, video monitors, voice control, and foot switches to guide robotic surgery.

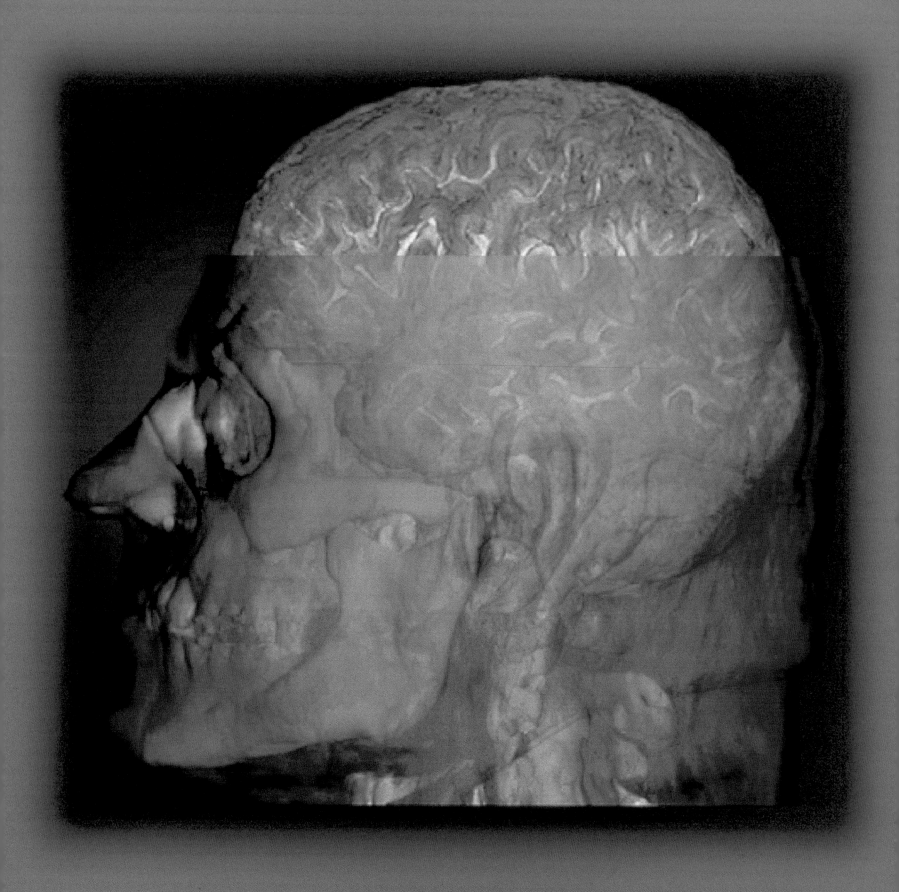

 **Norton's plane provides a lifeline to the poor in remote Tanzanian villages.**

▲ **A young AIDS patient prepares for his first flight.**

Mafinga, Tanzania

In his remote African village, Bill Norton has no telephone, electricity, or running water. But the Internet has helped him build an airplane that saves lives. Norton, a volunteer in Kibidula, purchased the airplane in kit form from Zenith Aircraft, a U.S.-based company. He credits his two-hour daily Internet connection, courtesy of the VITA (Volunteers in Technical Assistance) satellite that passes over each day, with helping him keep the airplane up and running. "Without radio connection to the satellite and the subsequent ability to send emails to Zenith, maintenance issues and operational support would be a nightmare," he says. Norton and his airplane play essential roles in getting supplies and medical relief to outlying villages.
Photographs by Arthur Berry

Two years ago, the Lawson family's perfect Hawaiian vacation became a nightmare when son Will suddenly fell ill. Then only two years old, Will was diagnosed with leukemia. From that moment on, the Lawsons have struggled to understand the trauma that continues to change their lives. Although the doctors help with medical advice, Lance Lawson found very little information on how the treatments felt from a patient's perspective. Instead of giving up, Lawson created Will's Page, a website where he chronicles the details of Will's struggle, from the pain and confusion of a bone-marrow transplant to the happy news of Will's regrowing hair. The website has drawn a wide response from families going through similar circumstances, who find valuable information at the site, and from people who have lived through leukemia, who offer support and advice. For Lawson, the site has played a large role in the healing process. "It keeps me from feeling so alone," he says.

Photographs by Patrick Tehan

"The sedative and pain medicine they used to give him for the procedure had made him sick.... He still has the rash on his cheeks. They said it appears to be just dry skin. It sure is hard to treat anything casually."

—*Will's Page, February 20, 1996*

▶ ▲ New York, New York, USA

What better medicine for a hospitalized child than a romp through a virtual playground with comedian Robin Williams?
It may not sound like traditional medical treatment, but Stephen Spielberg's Starbright Foundation uses advanced videoconferencing tools, fiber-optic phone lines, and a network of high-end PCs scattered around the country to help ease the pain of seriously ill children. On February 8, Robin Williams added his own magic to the mix and ventured into Starbright's four virtual realms, playing computer games with pediatric patients at the Mount Sinai Medical Center. While there, Williams met 16-year-old liver-transplant patient Chrissy Oriol, who found someone even more interesting when she and Williams went online: another child who had gone through the same operation and long recovery. The two patients could chat online about their experiences between game sessions with Williams. Oriol says the Starbright program was a welcome distraction. "I wasn't bored anymore," she says. "It was really, really cool."
Photographs by Gregory Heisler

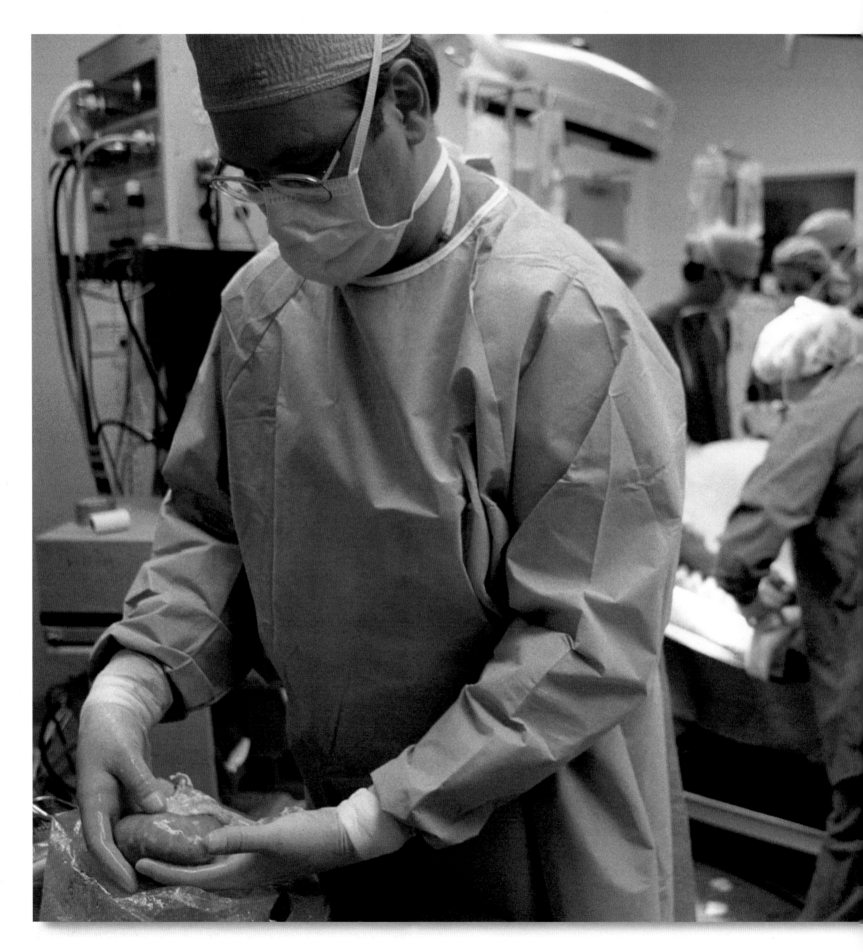

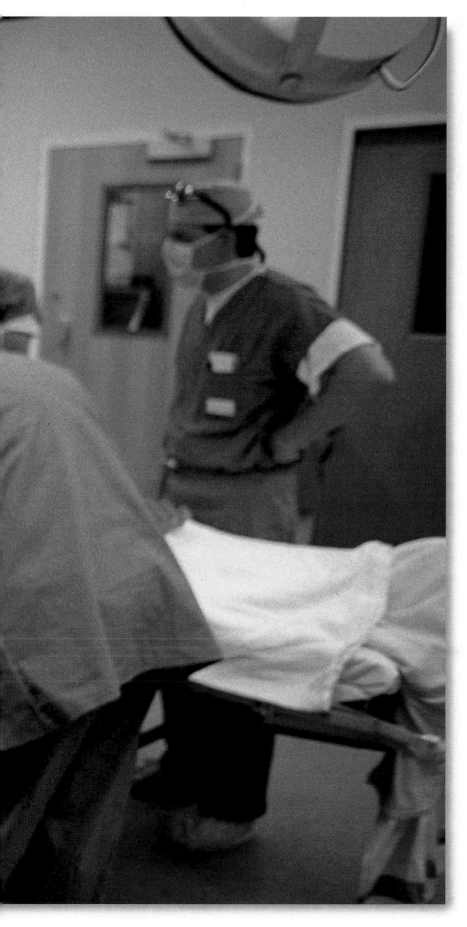

◀ ▲ Patient Tommy Frye waits unconscious on the operating table as a hospital worker carries the kidney that came to him via human kindness and cyberspace.

Charlottesville, Virginia, USA

There's a 12- to 18-hour window for success when it comes to matching organ donors with recipients. Until a year ago, the process involved a frantic series of phone calls and faxes around the country to find the right match. Typically, the coordinator would be able to place only two or three organs per donor within the crucial time frame. Though needed by many, organs such as the lungs and pancreas would rarely get placed because the coordinators ran out of time. Now, with the aid of Xpedite, a pilot project designed to transmit donor information electronically to all participating hospitals at once, the number of organs a coordinator can place has climbed to eight. Currently, the program is being tested by the Virginias Organ Procurement Agency (VOPA); so far, the agency has used the computerized system 25 times to place more than 100 organs.
Photographs by
William Campbell

▲ **Fredericksburg, Virginia, USA**

Special Agent Brad Smith coordinates an online program that posts the most wanted criminals in the world.
Photograph by Dick Swanson

▶ **Cairo, Egypt**

Special forces in Cairo practice "realistic reaction drills" in preparation for nabbing international terrorists.
Photograph by Barry Iverson

In the fight against international terrorism, cyberspace is a good place to hang Most Wanted posters. Heroes, a U.S. State Department counterterrorism program, uses the Net to penetrate the borders of countries suspected of harboring international terrorists and drug traffickers. Posting the names, aliases, photos and alleged crimes of suspected criminals on its website, the State Department entices informers and bounty hunters the world over with rewards of up to $4 million per capture. According to program coordinator Brad Smith, "The Internet is ideal for getting uncensored information to people where totalitarian governments still control the media." Already, Heroes has helped snare one of the men involved in the bombing of PanAm Flight 103, and another suspected of participating in the World Trade Center attack.

CLEARANCE 10FT 5IN

◀ Soldiers stand guard over the Cheyenne Mountain Operations Center's underground fortress.

▲ Dallas, Texas, USA

Cold-war missile-tracking systems from the 1960s have trickled down to the laptops used by today's Dallas bicycle cops to do background checks.
Photograph by Shelly Katz

◀ Peterson Air Force Base, Colorado, USA

Who knew 30 years ago that cold war technology would someday also be used to troll for space garbage? Behind the 25-ton, bomb-resistant door, the North American Aerospace Defense Command (NORAD) uses cybertechnology—such as radar, telescopes, and high-resolution videocameras—to keep continuous vigil over the 9,000 rocket parts and other flotsam that fill the heavens. Though a seemingly minor task, the repercussions of a collision between space debris, which travels at an estimated rate of 17,000 miles an hour, and a shuttle or satellite could be major—in 1983 a tiny orbiting paint chip badly damaged a shuttle window.
Photograph by Paul Chesley

▶ **John Hofsess started DeathNet, a website devoted to right-to-die discussions and materials.**

Victoria, Canada

After watching his 80-year-old mother die a slow, undignified death, John Hofsess created the DeathNet website, a home for honest dialogue about the most ignored fact of life. The site, which Hofsess claims has "the world's largest collection of 'right-to-die' materials and services on the Internet," has been honored with numerous national and international recognitions. It has also been a lightening rod for the international censorship debate swirling around the Net. Suicide-prevention activists have called for an outright ban of the site, arguing that the materials there might encourage depressed people to kill themselves. But by requiring site visitors to show proof of three months' membership in a right-to-die organization before they can order materials, Hofsess says that DeathNet has a more restrictive policy than most stores selling books like *Final Exit*, a primer on suicide. Despite the criticism, Hofsess sees a very real need for DeathNet: "The one indisputable human right is the right to say 'no more.'"

Photographs by Mark van Manen

▲ **Hofsess and Anita Bundy of Canada's Right to Die Society demonstrate an "exit bag" commonly used in assisted suicide.**

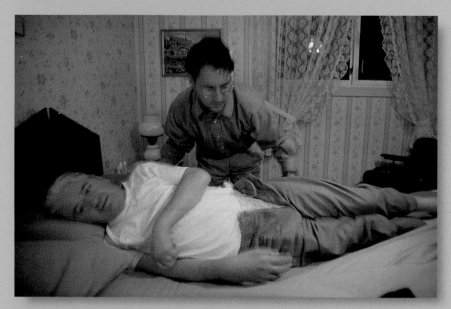

Even turning in bed required assistance for Austin Bastable, who suffered from multiple sclerosis.

▶ Austin Bastable turned to the Internet in his quest for a legal suicide.

▲ Windsor, Canada

Austin Bastable suffered from multiple sclerosis for 25 years. After a failed suicide attempt in November 1994, Bastable realized that any future attempts would require assistance—ideally, legal assistance. With the help of the Right to Die Society of Canada, Bastable established a website where he provided audio clips, family portraits, and links to other sites involved in the right-to-die debate. Bastable's site sparked considerable debate. The Campaign Life Coalition published a Save Austin Bastable Home Page on its LifeNet website. And he received so much "Christian love" email that he shut down his electronic mailbox. As his health grew weaker, Bastable vowed to continue his right-to-die fight. He wanted out of his misery: "When I was born, I cried and the world rejoiced. But when I die, if I get it right, the world will cry—and I will rejoice." *Epilogue:* On May 6, 1996, with right-to-die activist Dr. Jack Kevorkian in attendance, Bastable took his own life.

Photographs by J. Kyle Keener

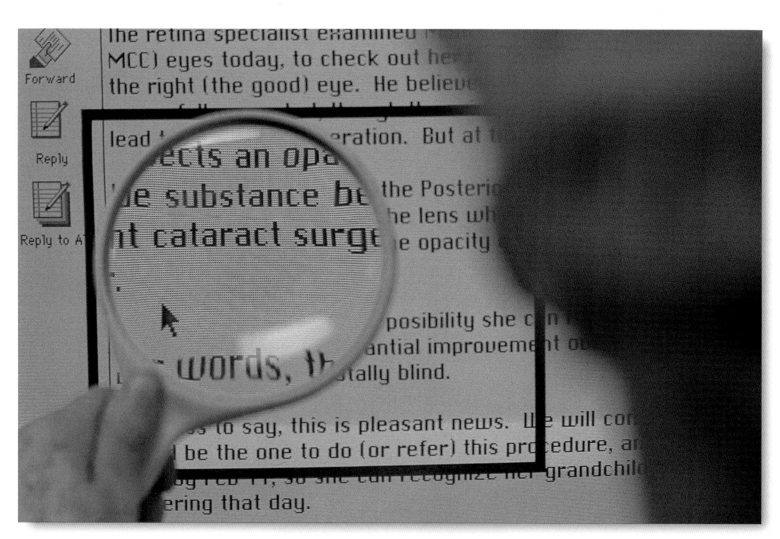

The retina specialist examined [...]
MCC) eyes today, to check out he[...]
the right (the good) eye. He believe[...]
lead [...] eration. But at t[...]
[...]ects an opa[...]
[...]e substance be[...] the Posterio[...]
[...]nt cataract surge[...]e opacity [...]
[...]e lens wh[...]
posibility she c[...]
[...]antial improveme[...]t o[...]
[...] words, t[...]tally blind.
[...]s to say, this is pleasant news. We will con[...]
[...] be the one to do (or refer) this procedure, ar[...]
[...]y reb 14, so she can recognize her grandchil[...]
[...]ering that day.

◀ ▲ **San Jose, California, USA**

For her 88th birthday, Roberta McClintic got wired, a gift from her two sons. Now 90, nearly blind, and confined to a wheelchair, McClintic stays in close touch with her family and a network of new friends online. As part of one of the fastest-growing demographic groups in cyberspace, McClintic is not alone—a fact that makes her very happy. "When I turned 90, I celebrated my birthday for 10 days and wore myself out, so I wasn't able to send any email. One sweet girl emailed my son to find out if I was all right." *Photographs by Jim Gensheimer*

▲ **Jerusalem, Israel**

The teachers at Gan Harmony School became concerned when three-year-old Moshe suddenly started regressing.

Joan Shrensky, founder of this unique school where disabled and nondisabled children share classrooms, was particularly puzzled: "Moshe has Williams syndrome, and while it's not uncommon for children with this disorder to stop progressing, it's rare that they would go backwards." Fortunately, Shrensky was able to tap into the Gan Harmony website, where she posted Moshe's case and asked for advice. Within days, her mind was at ease. Four parents of Williams syndrome children confirmed that this type of regression was rare but temporary. "Before the website, we had limited resources," says Shrensky. "Now, we're able to extend our reach. It's a wealth of information not only for us but for parents and communities everywhere."
Photograph by Ricki Rosen

◀ ▶ **Ellicot City, Maryland, USA**

Debbie McFadden arranged for surgery to straighten Tanya's legs; she is thrilled to have shoes for the first time in her life.
Photographs by Karen Kazmauski

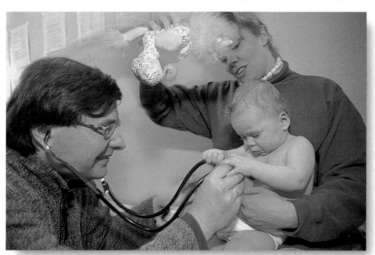

◀ **Moscow, Russia**

An International Children's Alliance client holds the baby she is adopting as he is examined by a Russian pediatrician.
Photograph by Jeremy Nicholl

Seven million children languish in orphanages throughout the former Soviet Union. One woman is using the Net to help them find homes. Debbie McFadden (left), founder of the International Children's Alliance, an agency that places children from Russia, China, and the Philippines, says that 1,000 inquiries about adoption are made per day on the Net. Some question the advisability of using the Internet to advertise adoptable children. McFadden disagrees: "Those who want to adopt children want to do it quickly. The Internet helps because with a few clicks of the mouse, anyone can be connected to a world of information." McFadden practices what she preaches. After years of helping other families, she adopted six-year-old Tanya, whom she found during a visit to a Russian orphanage. Tanya's parents had abandoned her because a tumor on her back had left her paralyzed. But for McFadden, it was love at first sight. "I'm like all other adoptive parents," she says softly. "I know that my being Tanya's mother was meant to be."

Into the Light

Countries represented:

Australia

Canada

England

India

Italy

Japan

Malaysia

Mexico

South Africa

USA

◀ **Port Alfred, South Africa**

Transporting his township into the digital age, this South African youth carries a donated monitor to the FNB Nemato Computer Lab.

The lab, located in the Nelson Mandela Township's police station in Port Alfred, was created through a combination of efforts—local and international, black and white. "The project has opened all sorts of doors," says Californian George Berhitoe, the lab's founder. "These kids have learned about computers, practiced their English, and corresponded via email about race relations and other subjects with students as far away as Malaysia, Australia, and Argentina."
Photograph by Mark Peters

Spiritus—*breath*—*is the root of* spirit. *It is synonymous with life force, with inspiration, and, for many religions, with notions of god. Spirit is the common denominator in the topics of this chapter: culture, religion, and education. The word* spirit *embodies the sum total of our aspirations. And spirit permeates cyberspace, in ways large and small.*

This sounds esoteric, but in fact spirit is a part of cyberspace because cyberspace is rapidly becoming an invisible part of ordinary, daily life. Given the novelty of cyberspace, one might expect its content to be bizarre. Instead, it is broad and deep, with virtually every aspect of human endeavor represented in the growing vastness of this online realm.

Spirit is most obvious online in the form of mainstream religious activity: Lubavitch Jews linking up over the World Wide Web, a Buddhist home page managed by a monk in Japan, and the Vatican's ambitious effort to publish rare literary treasures previously hidden from public view. Even the Dalai Lama has a presence on the Web. Cyberchurches have already appeared, and at the fringe, it is only a matter of time before we witness the appearance of something like the First Church of Hackers.

Spirit also takes more secular forms. Individuals fighting hate crimes and revolutionaries seeking social justice have found the Net to be a potent tool for their aspirations. Meanwhile, a bright but frustrated student in a remote Montana town finds challenge through home schooling on the Web.

These ventures into cyberspace will not be without surprises. The Prime Minister of Malaysia is determined to make his the most wired country in all of Asia. But what will his society think when it discovers that cyberspace-cruising Muslim women are gazing at half-dressed movie heartthrobs?

In the end, spirit will prevail, for cyberspace is an open-ended medium, as full of hope as it is of surprise. It is a shape shifter, opening our reality to a vast new digital horizon. And somewhere ahead in the light lies a new home for our aspirations and our humanity.—P.S.

▲ ▷ **Longreach, Australia**

The 70,000-acre sheep ranch in the Australian outback where Christene Capel lives is about as far from an urban university as she could imagine. Yet, as the first telecommuting student to electronically submit course material, Christene completed her degree in teacher-librarianship at Queensland University of Technology in Brisbane, 1,500 kilometers from her home. Now she's working on a master's degree in education. Her subject: remote use of computer-mediated communication. Capel admits that telecommuting has enlarged her world. "I never had any interest in a computer until I discovered it to be a communication tool. If you could picture where I live, you would realize why I am so excited about the prospects."
Photographs by John Marmaras

◀ ▲ **Sheffield, England**

Since a field trip into outer space was out of the question, these high school students in Sheffield, England, decided to explore the cosmos via cyberspace.
Thanks to the school's online link to Sheffield Hallam University Centre for Science Education, Westfield School students are exploring images from the Hubble telescope and downloading NASA graphics and data to help them build small-scale models of the solar system. "It's like dropping into a living library whenever and wherever you wish," says teacher Andy Bullough. "Imagine the cosmos being instantly available. The students don't even have to wait for darkness to fall."
Photographs by Dod Miller

Brooklyn, New York, USA

When Rabbi Yosef Kazen surfs the Web from his Brooklyn office, he sees a prophet's words coming true. As one of the developers behind an online learning center called Chabad-Lubavitch in Cyberspace, Rabbi Kazen sees the Internet, which was originally created as a cold war military tool, as "the fulfillment of Isaiah's prophecy that swords will be turned into plowshares." The website, primarily dedicated to the teachings of the orthodox Jewish sect, is a virtual temple that can attract a far larger and more diverse congregation than a traditional, physical temple could. "We could never be in touch with people in China, South Korea, Antarctica, and Turkey on a daily basis without this medium," says the rabbi. Given the rapidly growing number of emails the site receives from around the world, Rabbi Kazen is positive that the Internet can "transmit the depth and joy inherent in a Torah-true way of life."
Photographs by Andy Levin

▸ **Rabbi Zelig Katzman wears his *talit* (ceremonial shawl) and *tefilin* (headpiece containing scriptures) during the weekday prayer service at Congregation Lubavitch.**

◀ ▲ **Flathead Lake, Montana, USA**

Thirteen-year-old R. Lee Steffen wasn't happy in public school—his fast-moving mind felt stifled. To ease his discomfort, his father helped him find education online. Joining an estimated quarter-million U.S. students using the Internet for home schooling, R. Lee—or CybeRLee, as his father calls him—is now studying at the fledgling Athena Preparatory Academy, sponsored by Virtual Online University. From his home on the remote shores of Flathead Lake, he's creating a virtual 3-D model of ancient Athens and learning history, English, and computer programming in the process. Internet-based schooling has been his ticket to educational freedom. "I can learn about anything I choose. My resources are unlimited," R. Lee says.

Photographs by Jay Dickman

▲ **Kuala Lumpur, Malaysia**

Seventy-year-old Mahathir Mohamad, prime minister of Malaysia, may just be one of the most technically savvy politicians on earth. Not only does he have his own Web page, he also answers questions from his constituents live on the Internet. Mohamad hopes to thoroughly wire the former British colony by the year 2000.
Photograph by Tara Sosrowardoyo

◀ **Bangi, Malaysia**

Muslim students at Universiti Kebangsaan Malaysia lift the lid on Pandora's box as they check out a bare-chested Matthew Modine on Hollywood Online. In a society where head scarves and strict religious attitudes are the norm, the Internet can be a powerful and sometimes disruptive tool. Yet Malaysian Prime Minister Mahathir Mohamad believes the threat is minimal. "Although there will be more freedom," he says, "there is little likelihood that Asian countries of the future will adopt the Western style of unlimited freedom."
Photograph by Tara Sosrowardoyo

> "Thomas Jefferson understood that democracy depends upon the free flow of information."
>
> —*Bill Clinton*

▲ **Washington, D.C., USA**

On February 8, President Clinton signed the controversial Telecommunications Reform Act of 1996, saying that the legislation will "bring the future to our doorstep." As the first major reform in telecommunications law in 60 years, the act will open new forms of communication through telephones, televisions, and computers. But while the bill unshackles communications at large, a provision of the bill banning the online transmission of "indecent" material could serve to stifle electronic expression. Cybercitizens protested, citing the First Amendment—"Congress shall make no law . . . abridging the freedom of speech, or of the press." Throughout the Internet, blue ribbons and Web pages with black backgrounds signaled the protest.
Photograph by Bob McNeely

▶ **San Francisco, California, USA**

The staff of HotWired, one of the most popular online magazines, demonstrates the debilitating effect the Communications Decency Act could have on the digital revolution.
Photograph by Kim Komenich

△ ▷ **Washington, D.C., USA**

Armed with a digital camera, Second Lady Tipper Gore captures a historic moment as President Clinton prepares to sign the Telecommunications Reform Act of 1996.
Both the issues of the act and those of education are of special concern to Tipper Gore. As part of her assignment on February 8, Tipper also traveled to wired schools to document how the Internet is changing the face of education around the country. Later that day, Vice President and Tipper Gore were able to view the 24 Hours in Cyberspace website, where her pictures were published.
Top and right photographs by Ron Edmonds
Above photograph by Tipper Gore

▲ At a traditional fire ceremony, Reverend Fuji sends his prayers to the heavens. Over the Internet, he plans to send Buddha's teachings to the masses.

◀ Although Reverend Fuji studied for eight years in the United States and is now working to connect 3,000 Tendai Buddhist temples by email, he continues to follow traditional Buddhist practices. On the previous pages, saffron-robed Reverend Fuji joins his family—also monks— for a communal meal.

Kyushu, Japan

At the 500-year-old Konjoin Buddhist Temple, Reverend Koshun Fuji's monastic life spans both the deeply traditional and the profoundly modern. Reverend Fuji's day begins at 4 a.m., when he purifies himself under a waterfall outside the temple. Following sunrise chants, the monk's devotional duties turn from the earthly to the electronic as he crafts a website that he hopes will enlighten the world about Buddha's compassionate teachings. "Nowadays the world is falling seriously ill, but it is not too late for us to make changes," he says. "Tendai Buddhism would like to use the Internet as one of the great communication tools to bring peace to the world."
Photographs by Kaku Kurita

▶ Reverend Fuji demonstrates his home page-in-progress to a fellow monk.

> **"With this project, we are able to draw the world of learning closer together."**
>
> *—Father Boyle*

Vatican City, Italy

The Vatican Library houses more than 2 million books and 150,000 historical documents, some dating back to the second century. Fragile with age and rare beyond belief, these ancient tomes were available only to a relatively small group of scholars—until recently. That's when Father Boyle, a 71-year-old Benedictine monk and computer aficionado, decided to take the centuries-old manuscripts online. In addition to preserving the documents from theft or damage, the project also gives researchers all over the world a chance to view the world's oldest bible manuscript and a 15th-century version of Ptolemy's *Geography*. "With this project, we are able to draw the world of learning closer together," says Father Boyle. Already, researchers as far flung as Ohio and Rio de Janeiro have visited the virtual Vatican, taking advantage of age-old knowledge in the most modern way.

Photographs by Massimo Siragusa

▼ **The Vatican collection contains the world's oldest bible and rare manuscripts, such as this 13th-century text about birds.**

▲ **Toronto, Canada**

**Ernst Zuendel, a Nazi sympa-
thizer and webmaster, won a
landmark freedom-of-speech
case in Canada's Supreme
Court. Here, taking glory as
Canada's free-speech martyr,
he stands in front of a
cross inscribed with the words
freedom of speech. The Nazi
flag is his own design.**
*Photograph by Arabella Anna
Schwarzkopf*

**The byways of the information superhigh-
way course with messages not only of love
but also of hate.** While religious groups are
finding digital proselytizing an effective way
to reach devotees, so too are hate groups, such
as that of Ernst Zuendel, a self-proclaimed
dissident and author of a tract asserting that
the Holocaust never happened. The Simon
Wiesenthal Center, a Los Angeles-based
agency that fights anti-Semitic and other hate
groups, has requested that Internet access
providers refuse to serve sites such as Zuendel's.
A second group, called Nizkor (Hebrew for
"we remember") dedicates itself to exposing
the claims of Zuendel and other so-called
revisionists.

Jamie McCarthy helps run Nizkor (Hebrew for "we remember"), a website with a mission of rebutting neo-Nazi revisionists who deny the Holocaust. McCarthy shields his face because of threats Nizkor has received.

▲ **Although electronic censorship is most often linked with the transmission of "obscene" material, the threat posed by online hate groups looms just as large—if not larger.** Hilary Ostrov, McCarthy's partner at Nizkor, is concerned that hatemongers may be more persuasive in the glitzy context of the Web. "Coated with the patina of professionalism a Web page affords," she says, "the distortions and lies await the click of the unsuspecting reader."
Photograph by Ward Perrin

▶ **Toronto, Canada**

Zuendel, whose fervent admiration for Adolf Hitler is evident in his sprawling collection of Nazi images, claims that websites like his are "our training wheels to freedom" and will enable people to experience "global liberation through information."
Photograph by Joe Traver

Chiapas, Mexico

The Zapatista rebels of southern Mexico have a secret weapon—one that has caught the Mexican government by surprise. It's the Internet, and it allows the rebels to use words more effectively than most armies use tanks and artillery. The Zapatista website Ya Basta ("Enough Already") has attracted global attention from journalists and Web surfers. This kind of covert maneuvering in cyberspace has bypassed the government's efforts to gag dissent through brute force. Recently Zapatista supporters traveled to Chiapas, where they joined "peace brigades," placing themselves between Mexican soldiers and the Mayan peasants. In a nonviolent and very wired way, the Zapatistas have been able to bring ordinary citizens of the world into their extraordinary struggle.

Center photograph by Francisco Mata Rosas
All other photographs by Eniac Martinez Ulloa

◀ **Though life as a rebel—or even a family of rebels—means life with a hidden identity, the Zapatista website lets them bring world attention to their cause.**

▷ **The Zapatistas are committed to protecting "the innocents"— peasants who bear the brunt of the Mexican army's assault.**

> ## "Any technology which helps to bring news and imagery is very, very useful."
> —*His Holiness the Dalai Lama*

◀ **As sunset falls on Dharamsala, where the Dalai Lama resides in exile, a Buddhist monk chants and carries a prayer wheel. Thanks to the Net, his beliefs and those of the Dalai Lama can be heard in cyberspace.**

▲ **Dharamsala, India**

Knowing that there are no borders in cyberspace, the exiled spiritual and political leader of Tibet has taken his cause to the Internet. The website of the Dalai Lama provides everything from updates on the persecution of Buddhist nuns in Chinese-occupied Tibet to a personal message from the Dalai Lama himself. Before the Net, volunteers at the Toronto-based World Tibet Network News used to spend hours in front of a fax machine, sending news of this exiled leader and his government to interested parties around the globe. Now, the task of news dissemination takes minutes and reaches far more people at a fraction of the cost.
Photographs by Thomas L. Kelly

Behind the Scenes at Mission Control

An excerpt from *The Seybold Report on Desktop Publishing*

Edit teams worked around the clock to collect, edit, and publish 61 stories by the end of the 24-hour project.

The Associated Press's Neal Ulevich is dwarfed by the equipment that poured into Mission Control from the 50 corporate sponsors.

On February 8, 1996, in a breathtaking collision of photojournalism and technology, Against All Odds Productions, led by photographer Rick Smolan and his partner, Jennifer Erwitt, pulled off its latest daring project, 24 Hours in Cyberspace: Painting on the Walls of the Digital Cave. *We went to Mission Control to see for ourselves not only the content but also the process, to find out how this star-studded cast managed to pull off this feat.*

Collaborative demonstrations of technology are always interesting, but rarely are they staged in public without full dress rehearsals. This project not only broke new ground, it did so in full view of tens of thousands of people. Using a barely tested system stitched together at a breakneck pace just before the event, the sleep-deprived crew at Mission Control nevertheless managed to pull the site together and see it survive the deluge of millions poring through its pages, leaving their signatures behind. As Eric Schmidt, chief technology officer at Sun Microsystems, wryly noted, "This is R&D without a safety net."

No one can ever accuse Rick Smolan of being an underachiever. A former *Time*, *Life*, and *National Geographic* photographer, in the 1980s Smolan created the best-selling series of Day in the Life coffee-table books. Ever since 1992, when he produced *From Alice to Ocean: Alone Across the Outback*—the first coffee-table book to come with its own CD-ROM—Smolan's Against All Odds Productions has pushed the edge of photojournalism technology. Last year's superb *Passage to Vietnam*, for example, extended multimedia CD-ROMs to new heights of accessibility and elegance.

So when we got wind of Smolan's latest project, *24 Hours in Cyberspace*, we were curious. We found out that he and his team were going to use the Web to document the Web, inviting the whole world to upload their stories, photos, and signatures to create a snapshot of cyberspace. We became intrigued by his vision, and we were excited at the prospect of seeing, once again, the results of dozens of world-class photographers fanning out to their one-day assignments. But when we learned that, true to its name, Smolan's Against All Odds Productions was going to try to pull off this feat with a hastily constructed, barely tested system based on software that wasn't even finished—well, we just knew we wanted to be there to see it.

Primitive snapshot. This time, Smolan's team used the technology itself in an effort to document the effect the Internet is having on people's lives. He and Project Director Jennifer Erwitt, Director of Technology Tom Melcher, Director of Photography Karen Mullarkey, and Project Organizer Patti Richards dispatched more than 150 professional photographers across the globe to photograph and tell pictorial stories about how the Internet is changing people's lives. The focus of the project was to use photojournalism to put a human face on cyberspace.

Because the Internet is so new, Smolan's crew gave their effort a subtitle, *Painting on the Walls of the Digital Cave*, in ironic recognition that in years hence, this snapshot of cyberspace would no doubt appear as primitive as the paintings of prehistoric man.

Not only was the goal to produce a book and CD-ROM, but, to up the ante, Against All Odds decided to publish on the Web some of the images and stories the same day they had been gathered—effectively compressing the editing time from months down to minutes and hours, then pumping the stories back over the Internet to millions of potential viewers in near real time.

In some ways, the publishing model for the project is similar to broadcast journalism's: using the Internet as a way to "beam" taped coverage of an event quickly all over the world. The difference, though, is that viewers have complete control over the speed and sequence of the action and are able to play it over and over again in different ways if they like. For publishers wanting a peek at news reporting of the future, it was a very interesting experiment.

Snowballing support. To broaden interest in the project, Against All Odds invited schools around the world to participate. What began as a simple message emailed on a Friday to a few people quickly snowballed. In the end, more than 100 schools and thousands of amateur photographers participated, uploading their pages and photographs to judges who rated the submissions to determine prizewinners.

Big guns. The sheer size and scope of the project attracted close to 50 supporting companies, which donated or loaned an estimated $5 million in equipment, as well as scores of talented staff. Kodak, Sun Microsystems, and Adobe Systems served as primary corporate sponsors; additional support was provided by America Online, Netscape Communications, and more than a dozen other high-profile corporations.

Kodak provided 9,000 rolls of film, Photo CD scanners, and its new DC-50 digital cameras. Sun supplied servers, networking software, storage, and Internet security experience, as well as Java programming and systems integration services. Adobe provided Photoshop and PageMaker software, as well as staff to Mission Control, and donated PageMill and Acrobat software to schools.

Building the site. "Mission Control," where the Web pages were built, was a specially constructed, 6,000-square-foot space in San Francisco's South of Market area. When we arrived, it looked like a cross between a daily newspaper at deadline and the control room for a NASA space flight. The place was crawling with editors acting as reporters, analysts, and TV crews. Even a few "groupies" swarmed about recording the action—and being part of it. For many, seeing

Mission Control, located in San Francisco, looked like a cross between a newsroom at deadline and the control room at a NASA launch.

Paul Chinn/San Francisco Examiner

the finished product live on the Web, with each person working to produce the next additions to it, was an epiphany. Talk about immediate gratification—it was as if every story a reporter wrote for a newspaper were immediately published and distributed. And in the end, the whole experience was validated by dozens of feature stories on the project that ran on network evening news, National Public Radio, and ABC's "Nightline" program.

The plan. As material poured in from around the world, a team of 80 editors, programmers, and designers—per shift—busily integrated it into a website. To manage the chaos, Smolan's crew devised a careful workflow in advance: Custom Web layout software from NetObjects served as a front end to Illustra's object-oriented database, with gobs of Sun and PC-clone hardware (and a few Macs) thrown at the problem.

The website (www.cyber24.com) featured six themes. Each began with an essay written by a noted personality, complemented by photo-essays laid out like pages in a coffee-table book or a magazine like *Life*.

Six teams worked independently to create the six theme areas. Each "pod" team had a text editor, a photo editor, and a Photoshop technician. In addition, a Traffic pod routed photos to the amateur and professional queues, and a Table of Contents pod prepared the overall pages.

Collecting. All the photographers used Kodak slide film to capture images for the book and CD-ROM. In addition, some photographers in the field had digital cameras and were able to transmit images as electronic mail messages to Mission Control. Many also shot with Kodak color negative film, which, after developing, was digitized by portable Polaroid scanners.

Designing and editing. Thirty design templates were created in advance under the direction of Clement Mok. These templates were the raw elements utilized by a new Web publishing tool from NetObjects, which allowed the dynamic generation of finished Web pages by nondesigners.

As material began pouring in, judges examined the professionally shot photos, assigned them themes,

Project Director Rick Smolan appeared on "Nightline," which sent camera crews around the world and devoted an entire evening to covering *24 Hours in Cyberspace*.

J. Carl Ganter

Technical Director Tom Melcher directed the hardware and software teams.

and rated them. The images were stored in the Illustra database and assigned to specific pods.

The editorial team—consisting of top story and photo editors on loan from national and international publications—picked the photos and captions they wanted to use, then selected a page layout from the predesigned templates. Each editorial team also had a Photoshop technician—working on a fast Sun SPARCstation—to crop, size, and compress the photos.

Complementing many stories were audio interviews with the photographers done by National Public Radio commentators. As the audio was fed to Mission Control, it was digitized. This material was edited into audio clips that were then attached to the page spreads.

Publishing. Every 30 minutes, the NetObjects software swept through the mounting server and collected the new pages. It then rebuilt the entire website, not only adding new content but also testing and forging new hyperlinks. At

Tipper Gore, wife of the U.S. vice president, participated as one of the *24 Hours in Cyberspace* photographers.

Mission Control, the *24 Hours* website rotated among five Sun Netra servers. But each half-hour, as the site was revised, it was copied to "mirror" sites around the globe.

Avoiding gridlock. Successful sites are sometimes punished for attracting too much attention— your humble server is likely to be swamped by a sea of surfers cruising for something neat to look at. One way to reduce a server's load is by mirroring—that is, copying the website to other machines and redirecting some traffic to those sites.

The *24 Hours* project was one of the largest tests of mirroring to date. It received in excess of 4.5 million hits in 24 hours—a

tremendous amount of traffic. The mirroring, set up by Sun, included three U.S. sites: Sun's headquarters in Mountain View, California; MCI in Atlanta; and BBN Planet in Rockville, Maryland. Internationally, the Internet World Exposition automatically funneled the material to its eight servers located around the world. These servers, connected by very high-speed, 45Mbps dedicated pipelines, effectively tripled the Internet's international capacity on that day.

As with all best-laid plans, however, these efforts to avoid gridlock broke down at times. On the West Coast, the Net nearly comes to a screeching halt every day at about 3 p.m. PST—just when Easterners go home and fire up their America Online browsers. Toward late afternoon on the 8th, access to the *24 Hours* site slowed to a crawl more than once, which made updates to the live site difficult.

A grand experiment. At the end of the day, the *24 Hours* project uplifted the spirits of all who worked on it and of those who dialed in to check it out. It is difficult to tune in to any Rick Smolan project and not leave it with a smile; this unassuming man and his work breed an enthusiasm that is highly contagious. In previous assignments, Smolan's team has traveled to many places, but in this one they touched the far corners of the globe all at once. ∎

—Excerpted with permission from an article in the February 19, 1996, issue of The Seybold Report on Desktop Publishing, *written by Craig Cline in San Francisco and Mark Walter in Media, Pennsylvania.*

Project Toolbox

Eastman Kodak
9,000 rolls of Kodak film
Kodak DC-50 and DCS-420 digital cameras
Kodak dye-sublimation printers
Kodak Digital Science Photo CD Imaging Workstation
Kodak Access software
Kodak Ektaprint 90 copier

Sun Microsystems
60 Sun SPARC and UltraSPARC workstations
Sun SPARC 1000 servers
Sun RAID disk arrays
Sun Netra servers
Sun Firewall-1 security software
Sun Microsystems mirror sites
Sun systems integration

Adobe Systems
Adobe Photoshop
Adobe PageMill
Adobe Acrobat
Adobe Illustrator
Adobe SiteMill
Adobe SuperATM
Adobe Font Library

America Online simulcast technology
America Online email

Netscape Navigator 2.0 software
Netscape Server software

MFS Communications voice and data communications
MFS Asynchronous Transfer Mode (ATM) network
MFS MAE East and West connectivity
Illustra multimedia database
Power Computing Mac OS systems
NEC Versa 4000 notebook computers
NEC PowerMate PCs
NEC MultiSync monitors
NetObjects Tools
A&I processing for Kodachrome and E6

Adaptive Solutions PowerShop boards
Apple Powerbooks
Associated Press transmission sites
Bay Networks hubs
BBN Planet mirror site
Best Power UPS
CE Software QuickMail
Cisco Systems routers
Claris Em@iler program
Dallas Semiconductor data rings
Digital Pond large-format image printing /reproduction services
Farallon Netopia internet routers
Farallon fast Ethernet hubs
Farallon EtherWave
FWB hard-disk storage and CD writers
Graham Technology Solutions systems integration
Herman Miller Aeron chairs
InternetMCI peering

Light Source Ofoto software
MegaHertz PCMCIA modems
MCI mirrror site
Newer Technology RAM
NOW Software Uptodate
Odwalla beverages
Power Foods Powerbars
Polaroid SprintScan scanners
Progressive Networks Real Audio technology
Proxima high-end portable projectors
SanDisk solid-state PCMCIA hard disks
Sonic Solutions digital audio software
Sonic MediaNet network
Spider Island Software TeleFinder BBS
Splash Technology PostScript card
Symantec MORE 3.1
Telos Systems phone interfaces
Telex headsets
Teralinx by Cyberports for Business
The Software Construction Company Photoshop plug-in
US Robotics modems
Visioneer Paperports
1996 World Exposition mirror sites
Wildfire Communications intelligent personal phone services
Xerox MajestiK color copier
ZZYZX digital transparencies

Photographer's Biographies

Joey Abraityte, Russia
Born in Vilnius, Lithuania, in 1974, Abraityte has worked as a freelance photographer based in Moscow since 1992.

Neil Alexander, USA
Alexander has been a merchant seaman, producer of television documentaries, and photojournalist. His photographs will be featured in two books in 1996: *Something Old, Something New*, a profile of food and culture in Louisiana, and *The University District*, a new volume in a series about the architecture of New Orleans.

Sedat Aral, Turkey
In his 12 years as a photojournalist, Aral has covered breaking-news stories throughout the Middle and Far East, as well as the former Soviet Union. He has worked internationally with Reuters, *Asiaweek*, JB Pictures, and SIPA Press.

Ragnar Axelsson, Iceland
An eight-time winner of the Icelandic Photojournalist award, Axelsson's photographs and picture essays have appeared in *Life, National Geographic, Le Figaro*, and other international publications. He has been on staff with *Morgunbladid*, Iceland's largest newspaper, since 1976.

Ricardo Azoury, Brazil
Brazil-born Azoury has been a photojournalist since 1977. His work has been published internationally in *Manchete, Time, Scientific American*, and *The Sunday Telegraph*. He is currently producing several CD-ROMs on Brazil.

Joe Baraban, USA
Houston-based Baraban brings a strong graphic style to his corporate advertising assignments. For 25 years, he has photographed worldwide for clients such as Philip Morris, Toyota, and Coca-Cola.

Pablo Bartholomew, India
Affiliated with Gamma-Liaison, Bartholomew has twice won World Press awards. His photographs have appeared in publications worldwide, including *The New York Times, The Sunday Times Magazine, Paris-Match, Geo*, and *National Geographic*, and have been exhibited internationally.

Nicole Bengiveno, USA
Based in New York, award-winning freelance photographer Bengiveno has photographed Soviet Central Asia and Albania for *National Geographic* and participated in the Day in the Life book series since 1980. Her work appears regularly in *U.S. News & World Report*.

Wesley Bocxe, Bosnia
A two-time Picture of the Year winner, Bocxe has covered stories in Africa, Bosnia, the Middle East, and Central and South America for publications such as *Time, Newsweek*, and *The New York Times*.

Enrico Bossan, Italy
In 1987 Bossan won the Kodak prize for professional photographers. His pictures have been published worldwide and exhibited at the Houston Photofest, and in Amsterdam; Tokyo; and Thessaloniki, Greece. Bossan has worked for Agenzia Contrasto since 1990.

Torin Boyd, Japan
Boyd began his career photographing for surfing magazines and is now a contract photographer in Tokyo for *U.S. News & World Report*. Boyd has participated in seven Day in the Life books.

Adrian Bradshaw, China
Bradshaw's academic background in Chinese and economics led him to move to China in 1984. Since then he has worked on assignments for major newsmagazines and for corporate clients. Of current trends he asks, "Now the waking dragon is wired—what next?"

Michael Bryant, USA
A winner of several regional Photographer of the Year awards and runner-up for the national POY award, Bryant has participated in four Day in the Life projects. His photograph is featured on the cover of *A Day in the Life of Ireland*.

Pablo Cabado, Argentina
Cabado's photographs have been exhibited in Central and South America, Europe, the United States, and cyberspace. Among his awards is the *Mother Jones* International Documentary Photography honor, and his work has been published in *Life, Mother Jones, Facts*, and elsewhere.

William Campbell, USA
The recipient of World Press and National Press Photographers Association awards, Campbell covers social and environmental issues for *Time* and other leading publications. Formerly based in Africa, Campbell now lives in the foothills of the Blue Ridge Mountains.

Matt Carr, Czech Republic
For the past two years, Carr has worked as a photographer for the *Prague Post* in the Czech Republic. While majoring in photojournalism at Ball State University, he worked at the *South Bend (Indiana) Tribune*.

Aaron Chang, USA
Chang is a veteran of six Day in the Life books. A senior photographer for *Surfing* magazine, he is currently producing and directing the surfing documentary *Carving Water*.

Gary Chapman, USA
A freelance photographer living in Atlanta, Chapman has photographed worldwide and has been published in *Life, Geo*, and *National Geographic*, as well as seven Day in the Life books. He and his wife, Vivian, are currently producing computer illustrations for the Image Bank.

Peter Charlesworth, Thailand
Based in Bangkok, Charlesworth has covered many of the world's fastest-growing economies for over a decade. His ceaseless travels around the region result in work published in *Time, Newsweek, The New York Times*, and other leading publications.

Paul Chesley, USA
A freelance photographer based in Aspen, Colorado, Chesley has completed dozens of assignments for *National Geographic, Life, Geo*, and other leading publications. Chesley has worked on 13 Day in the Life books, and his solo exhibitions have appeared in museums worldwide.

Pedro Coll, Spain
Coll abandoned a career as a lawyer at age 28 to pursue photography. He has contributed to many Day in the Life books. His own book, *El Detenido: La Habana (Havana: Locked in Time)*, was recently published by Lunwerg Editores.

Charlie Cortez, USA
A staff photographer for the *Elmira (New York) Star-Gazette*, Cortez has won the New York Associated Press award for portrait photography. He is an active member of the National Association of Hispanic Journalists and the National Press Photographers Association.

Guglielmo de' Micheli, Italy
De' Micheli is a freelance photojournalist whose work regularly appears in major U.S. and European publications. A contributor to many Day in the Life books, his work in *A Day in the Life of Ireland* earned him an Award of Excellence from *Communication Arts*.

Arnaud de Wildenberg, France
A two-time World Press prizewinner, lawyer-photographer de Wildenberg has covered international news stories for *Time, Stern, Paris-Match*, and other leading magazines. Currently concentrating on freelance feature stories and corporate assignments, he is affiliated with Gamma and Sygma.

Jay Dickman, USA
A Pulitzer Prize–winning photographer, Dickman is a contributor to *National Geographic, Time, Life, Fortune*, and *Forbes*, among others.

At the Cosmonautic School in Siberia, a student grows food for a yearlong "cybermission" to Mars. (p. 88)

Nikolai Ignatiev

An actress prepares for her appearance in Union Squared, a cybersoap found only on the Web. (p. 104)

Nicole Bengiveno

On his website, Ernst Zeundel calls himself a free-speech martyr and claims the Holocaust never happened. (p. 200)

Joe Traver

Brad Doherty, USA
Doherty worked as a staff photographer for the *Daily Texan* at the University of Texas, Austin, and was a photography intern for the *Quincy (Massachusetts) Patriot-Ledger* and the *Colorado Springs Sun.*

Don Doll, S.J., USA
A Jesuit priest and Creighton University professor in Omaha, Nebraska, Doll's photography has been featured in *National Geographic* and several Day in the Life books. He created *Crying for a Vision*, a book about the Lakota nation in South Dakota.

Elena Dorfman, USA
A finalist for a Fulbright creative grant, Dorfman is the author of *The C-Word: Teenagers and Their Families Living with Cancer* (Newspaper Press, 1994) and *When Learning is Tough* (Albert Whitman, 1994).

Misha Erwitt, USA
New York native Erwitt began taking pictures at age 11. His work has been published in major U.S. magazines, and he has participated in eight Day in the Life books. He is now on the staff of *The New York Daily News.*

David Falconer, USA
A staff photographer for *The Oregonian* for 25 years, Falconer now works on freelance assignments for *National Geographic, Sunset, People,* and Northwest Airlines. An award-winning travel photographer, his work was included in the *National Geographic Society 100* yearbook.

Melissa Farlow, USA
An award-winning photographer and teacher, Farlow has participated in several Day in the Life books and regularly works for *National Geographic.* She documented several African families for *Women in the Material World,* a book comparing women in different cultures.

Dana Fineman, USA
Fineman's participation in the Day in the Life project in Hawaii brought many new opportunities. Since then, she has had a "really wonderful, successful career." She is most proud of her contributing-photographer position at *Life* magazine.

Eugene Fisher, USA
Fisher's work has been featured in many esteemed publications worldwide, including *Smithsonian, Geo,* and *Stern,* and has been exhibited in the United States and Canada. He has also received numerous awards and honors, as well as recognition in *Communication Arts'* Photo Annual.

Loren Fisher, USA
An award-winning photographer and photo editor, Fisher edited and published *Pope John Paul II: An American Celebration,* in which 12 photographers and three writers documented the 1995 U.S. papal visit, and contributed to *Branson Backstage.*

Natalie Fobes, USA
A Pulitzer Prize finalist and recipient of the Alicia Patterson Foundation grant, Fobes contributes to many leading publications. Her book, *Reaching Home: Pacific Salmon, Pacific People,* has won numerous awards. Seattle-based Fobes is working on several book and CD-ROM projects.

J.B. Forbes, USA
A Pulitzer Prize finalist for his coverage of the Mexico City earthquake in 1986, Forbes' work has appeared in major news and feature magazines. Since 1975 Forbes has worked for the *St. Louis Dispatch,* where he is now director of photography.

Bill Frakes, USA
A contract photographer for *Sports Illustrated,* Frakes has participated in several Day in the Life books. He was on the *Miami Herald* photographic staff when it won a Pulitzer Prize in 1992.

Raphael Gaillarde, France
A leading photographer with Gamma-Liaison, Gaillarde's photographs have appeared in *Paris-Match, Geo,* and other major magazines in Europe. Among his several World Press awards is the prestigious Oskar Barnack prize.

John Gapps III, USA
Gapps was born in Oklahoma City and has worked for the Associated Press for the past 10 years doing general-assignment and combat photography.

Jim Gensheimer, USA
An award-winning staff photojournalist for the *San Jose Mercury News,* Gensheimer has contributed to *A Day in the Life of California* and several other photography books. In 1995 he became the first American newspaper photojournalist to visit North Korea since the Korean War.

Paul F. Gero, USA
Now a staff photographer for *The Arizona Republic/Phoenix Gazette,* Gero covered the 1988 political campaigns of four major candidates. He has spent a significant amount of time in Mexico documenting immigration issues and the Tarahumara Indians in the Chihuahua highlands.

Rob Goebel, USA
Winner of three regional Picture of the Year awards, Goebel is currently on the staff of the *Indiana Star/News.* Eleven of the Ball State University graduate's photographs have been included in several Best of Photojournalism books.

John Gollings, Australia
Gollings' architectural photography is characterized by strong formal composition and reflects the technical resources and craft skills the discipline requires.

David Gottschalk, USA
A staff photographer for the *Arkansas Democrat-Gazette* since 1990, Gottschalk began his career at the *Plano (Texas) Star Courier* after graduating from the University of Nebraska, Omaha, in 1985.

Bill Greene, USA
Among his many honors, Greene was named Photographer of the Year in 1987 and Boston Press Photographer of the Year seven times. He also won the World Press prize for his coverage of the 1993 Midwest floods.

Judy Griesedieck, USA
Minneapolis-based Griesedieck is a freelance photographer whose work has appeared in *Time, U.S. News & World Report, Newsweek, People,* and *USA Today.* She has participated in several photography books, including four Day in the Life projects.

Stan Grossfeld, USA
An associate editor for the *Boston Globe,* Grossfeld received Pulitzer Prizes in 1984 and 1985. He has won the Canon Photo Essay award, the Overseas Press award, the Lowell Thomas award, and the UNICEF Local Hero award.

Louise Gubb, South Africa
For the past decade, Gubb's work has focused on the struggle against apartheid in South Africa and Nelson Mandela's presidency. Prior to that she was based in New York, covering such stories as the changes in China and the Ethiopian famine.

Dirck Halstead, USA
Now *Time* magazine's senior White House photographer, Halstead began his career at age 17 covering the Guatemalan revolution. Since then, he has traveled worldwide for UPI and *Time.* Halstead is producing special reports on the 1996 U.S. presidential campaign for *Time's* website.

Acey Harper, USA
Since being on the start-up staff of *USA Today,* Harper has traveled worldwide for clients such as *People, National Geographic,* and *Time.* He has won numerous awards for photography and photo editing. He lives in Tiburon, California, and in cyberspace.

Mark Edward Harris, USA
In his long career, Harris has traveled extensively and won numerous awards, including a Clio for print advertising and an Ace for directing and producing television videos. He is working on a book documenting the great names in photography.

Gregory Heisler, USA
Best known for his trademark editorial covers and essays for *Time, Life,* and *The New York Times,* Heisler is also an award-winning advertising photographer. Among the kudos he has received are the World Image award and the Leica Medal of Excellence.

Andy Hernandez, Russia
A contract photographer with *Newsweek* since 1984, Hernandez has covered the world's hot spots, including the Tienanmen Square massacre, the bombing of Baghdad, Iraq during the Gulf War, and the collapse of the Soviet Union.

Bill Hess, USA
Hess flies a small plane across the Far North, documenting the cultures of the rural and native peoples in Alaska, Canada, Greenland, and the Russian Far East. Founder of Running Dog Publications, his credits include *National Geographic* and *Geo*.

David Hiser, USA
An outdoor-oriented editorial photographer and photo educator, Hiser's award-winning work has appeared in *National Geographic, Audubon,* and *Life*. His images of an endangered hunter-gatherer culture in Borneo can be seen in *Penan: Nomads of the Dawn*.

Filip Horvat, Croatia
Croatian-born Horvat has been covering the Balkan war and breaking news worldwide, and his work appears regularly in international magazines. He won Picture of the Year in 1995, and in 1990 he cofounded SABA Press Photos with Marcel Saba.

Nikolai Ignatiev, Russia
Ignatiev was born in Moscow and served in the Soviet Army in Afghanistan as a military interpreter from 1977 to 1979. Ignatiev took up photography in 1982 and had his first published picture in *Newsweek* in 1984. Although now based in Britain, he returns regularly to Russia on assignments.

Einar Falur Ingolfsson, Iceland
Born in Iceland, Ingolfsson received his masters in fine arts in photography from the School of Visual Arts in New York in 1994. Since 1992 he has worked for *Morgunbladid,* Iceland's largest newspaper, as photographer, writer, and picture editor.

Barry Iverson, Egypt
Based in Cairo, Iverson has covered the Middle East and Africa for *Time* and other clients since 1979. In 1985, he was awarded a Fulbright grant that resulted in a book, *Comparative Views of Egypt*.

Ron Johnson, USA
The recipient of several regional Photographer of the Year awards, Johnson has been a staff photographer for the *LaCrosse (Wisconsin) Tribune* since 1985.

Katsumi Kasahara, USA
Kasahara has been an Associated Press Tokyo staff photographer since 1977. He has covered many Olympic events in his career, including those in Seoul, Calgary, Albertville, and Lillehammer, and won a News Photo Award in 1985. He uses digital cameras in his work.

Ed Kashi, USA
Since 1991, Kashi has been working with *National Geographic,* specializing in Middle East issues. His cover story on the Kurds resulted in a book, *When the Borders Bleed*. Kashi's latest project focuses on the life of Jewish settlers in the West Bank.

Karen Kasmauski, USA
Since 1984, Kasmauski has traveled worldwide as a contract photographer for *National Geographic,* where her April 1995 story on Ho Chi Minh City appeared on the cover. She also photographed the book *Hampton Roads* (Howell Press).

Shelly Katz, USA
Katz has covered every major U.S. presidential candidate since 1959, numerous presidential inaugurations, wars, riots, earthquakes, and turmoil in the Middle East. He has been a contract photographer for *Time* and participated in several Day in the Life projects.

Bill Keay, Canada
Keay has been a staff photographer with the *Vancouver Sun* for 21 years. He is the recipient of six Canadian Press awards for feature photography and the British Columbia Newspaper award for feature photography.

J. Kyle Keener, USA
A four-time winner of the regional Photographer of the Year award, Keener has traveled extensively covering AIDS in Uganda, Nelson Mandela's release from prison in South Africa, and ethnic violence in Rwanda. He is a staff photographer for the *Detroit Free Press*.

Beth A. Keiser, USA
Currently a staff photographer at the Associated Press, in the past two years Keiser has covered such major events as the Oklahoma City bombing and the Pan American Games in Argentina, as well as the Super Bowl and NBA finals. A graduate of the University of Miami, Keiser was formerly with *The Miami Herald*.

Thomas L. Kelly, Nepal
Much of Kelly's work concerns the culture of his adopted country. The most recent of his five books is *Tibet: Reflection from the Wheel of Life* (Abbeville Press, 1993). In mid-1995 he produced and designed two Internet multimedia stories for *Wired* magazine.

Nick Kelsh, USA
A veteran of several Day in the Life projects, Kelsh is the first to be honored with the covers of more than one book— he has four. His work has appeared in *Newsweek, Life, National Geographic, Geo,* and other major magazines.

Douglas Kirkland, USA
Kirkland established himself at *Look* and *Life* magazines in the 1960s and '70s after apprenticing with Irving Penn. A book of his work, *Light Years,* was published in 1989. In 1995 he was given an S.O.C. Lifetime Achievement award.

Roberto Koch, Italy
Koch's photographs have been exhibited internationally and published widely in the world press. *Istanti di Russia,* a collection of his best work in Russia, won the Kodak prize for photography in 1988. A Ph.D. in electronics, Koch founded the Contrasto agency.

Kim Komenich, USA
San Francisco Examiner staff photographer Komenich received the 1987 Pulitzer Prize for his coverage of the Philippine revolution. His work has appeared in *Life, Newsweek, Time,* and other magazines, and he has taught advanced documentary photography for nine years.

Steve Krongard, USA
Award-winning photographer Krongard lives in a 1790 farmhouse outside of New York City. He shoots in his SoHo studio, as well as around the world, for a variety of corporate clients in the airline, technology, banking, and other industries.

Kaku Kurita, Japan
Kurita began his career as a commercial photographer, but at the Tokyo Olympics in 1964, he turned to photojournalism. Since then, he has become one of Japan's most successful international photojournalists. He has been with Gamma-Liaison in Tokyo for 22 years.

Petri Kurkaa, Australia
After spending five years as an assistant/photographer, Kurkaa went freelance in 1994, working primarily with newspapers and magazines. His education consisted of two years of art school in the photo-media department.

Jean Pierre Laffont, France
Laffont is a founding member of Gamma USA and Sygma. Among his awards are those from the New York Newspaper Guild and the Overseas Press Club, as well as the Madelein Dane Ross award. His work appears regularly in the world's leading magazines.

Frederick Larson, USA
A photojournalist for the *San Francisco Chronicle* for 17 years, Larson has received more than 50 awards, including the 1994 National Press Photographers/Nikon Sabbatical grant for the story "Heroes: The Changing Faces of American Manhood." He also teaches documentary photography.

Olivier Laude, France/USA
A freelance photographer, Laude has traveled extensively throughout Asia, Europe, and North and Central America. He is the publisher and creative director of @tlas, an acclaimed online magazine of photography, design, multimedia, and illustration. Born in France, he lives in San Francisco.

Sarah Leen, USA
Leen's work appears regularly in *National Geographic,* and she has participated in six Day in the Life books. She has been an instructor at the Missouri Photo Workshop for four years and taught at the Maine Photographic Workshop in summer 1995.

Andy Levin, USA
Levin is a contributing photographer at *Life*. A participant in 10 Day in the Life books, he has won awards from the Art Directors Club and the National Press Photographers Association. His whimsical look at Coney Island was the cover story of *Reportage*.

Reiko Chiba, the first Japanese pop star with a cyberspace presence, signs autographs for fans. (p. 129)

Flanked by his proud parents, Mark Robbins prepares to wed the true love he met online. (p. 114)

Malcolm Linton, Great Britain
Affiliated with Black Star, Linton was wounded twice while covering wars in El Salvador and the former Soviet republic of Georgia. Based in Nairobi, Kenya, he won the 1994 Picture of the Year for his story "Georgia at War."

R. Ian Lloyd, Singapore
Lloyd has been based in Singapore since 1980. He formed his own company, R. Ian Lloyd Productions, in 1983 and has since photographed more than 28 books on Asia. His award-winning photography has appeared on the covers of *Newsweek, Fortune, Travel Holiday, National Geographic Traveler, Gourmet,* and *Business Week.*

David Loh, Malaysia
Loh has worked as a professional photographer for the past five years. He has been with Reuters in Kuala Lumpur for the past year. He had his first solo exhibition in 1993, entitled "Fragments of an Arrival."

Bill Luster, USA
Luster has shared in two Pulitzer Prizes: one for feature photography in 1976, and one for local reporting in 1988. He has been the Kentucky News Photographer of the Year five times. He is a past president of the National Press Photographers Association, and former chair of the NPPA Flying Short Course, one of the nation's premier photojournalism seminars. He is currently the administrator of the NPPA/Nikon Documentary Sabbatical grant program.

Sandra Markle, USA
Markle is an author and photographer specializing in science and nature.

John Marmaras, Australia
Marmaras has contributed to four Day in the Life projects. He has had extensive experience both in magazine and corporate photography. Marmaras is now based in Sydney.

Bullit Marquez, Philippines
Marquez started his photography career in 1984 and has been connected with the Associated Press for 12 years. He has covered events in the Philippines and most parts of Asia since 1984.

Eniac Martinez Ulloa, Mexico
Martinez Ulloa studied at the International Center of Photography and the Cuban Superior Institute of Art. His photographs have been exhibited in Mexico, the United States, and Europe. One of these exhibits was for the winners of the *Mother Jones* Documentary Photography competition, shown in the Ansel Adams Center for Photography in San Francisco. In 1989 Martinez Ulloa was awarded first prize in the *Mother Jones* international competition, and a Fulbright grant for creative work.

Francisco Mata Rosas, Mexico
Mata Rosas worked at the Mexican newspaper *La Jornada* from 1986 to 1991, and his photographs have been published internationally and exhibited in Mexico and Europe. In 1989 he won the Honor Prize in the Commemorative Concourse at the Bicentenary of the French Revolution, and a production grant from the Mexican National Advisory for Culture and the Arts.

Jim McHugh, USA
McHugh has shot dozens of cover stories for such publications as *Life, People, Entertainment Weekly,* and *The London Times.* In 1990 he coauthored, with museum director Henry Hopkins, *California Artists: New Works* (Chronicle Books), which received the coveted Golden Quill award that year. McHugh is currently working with the National Academy of Recording Artists on a book about the Grammy awards.

William Mercer McLeod, USA
San Francisco–based McLeod is primarily an editorial photographer, shooting for publications such as *Rolling Stone, Wired, Premiere,* and *Entertainment Weekly.*

Joe McNally, USA
McNally, a former copy boy at *The New York Daily News,* was described by *American Photo* as "perhaps the most versatile photojournalist working today" and was listed as one of the 100 most important people in photography in 1993. *Life* magazine hired him in 1994 as its first staff photographer in more than 20 years. He has contributed to many Day in the Life projects and was a featured exhibitor at the 1991 Festival of Photojournalism in Perpignan, France. McNally resides in Westchester, New York.

Bob McNeely, USA
McNeely currently serves as the director of White House Photographic Services and as President Bill Clinton's personal photographer. His photographic career began in the United States Army while he was an infantryman in Vietnam. His work has appeared in national and international publications, including *The New York Times, Newsweek, Time, Vogue,* and *Life.*

Daniel Meadows, Great Britain
Meadows is probably best known for his traveling photo studio in a converted double-decker bus (1974–75). He is a photographer and teacher of photographers. In 1994 he set up a new postgraduate program in photojournalism at Cardiff University, where he now teaches.

Doug Menuez, USA
Menuez coproduced *15 Seconds: The Great California Earthquake of 1989,* a book that raised over a half-million dollars for earthquake victims. His work has appeared in six Day in the Life books, and in *The Power to Heal, Circle of Life,* and *The African Americans.* In 1987 Menuez founded Reportage, an agency specializing in black-and-white photojournalism for corporations. In 1993 he published *Defying Gravity: The Making of Newton,* which won the gold medal in the *Photo District News* Photo/Design contest.

Claus C. Meyer, Brazil
In 1985 *Communications World* selected Meyer as one of the top annual-report photographers in the world. His excellence in color photography has been recognized by Kodak and Nikon, and in 1981 he won a Nikon International Grand Prize. He has published several books on Brazil; his most recent is a book on the Amazon (1993).

Pedro Meyer, Mexico
Meyer is one of Latin America's most prominent photographers. He has also contributed significantly to bridging the transition between traditional photography and digital-image making. *Aperture* recently published a book of his digital images under the title *Truths & Fictions.* In 1991 The Voyager Company published his CD-ROM entitled *I Photograph to Remember,* which contained images and narration documenting the last years of his parents' lives. He is currently producing an Internet website, called zonezero, which is dedicated to the work of other photographers.

Dod Miller, Great Britain
Born in the United Kingdom in 1960, Miller grew up in the former Soviet Union, the United States, and South Africa. In the mid-'80s he started freelancing for *The London Times* and later for the *Observer.* He joined Network Photographers in 1993. He is currently working on various advertising commissions.

Dario Mitidieri, Great Britain
Mitidieri was among the first journalists to cover the earthquake in Kobe, Japan, in 1995. He produced a photographic project about the street children of Bombay, India, after winning the W. Eugene Smith Memorial Grant in Humanistic Photography in 1992. Among his other awards are the Visa d'Or and the Premio Fotografia Periodistica la Nacion. His work has been exhibited throughout Europe.

David Modell, Great Britain
Modell won the World Press award in 1993 for sports stories, and the 1994 World Press Master Class. Since the age of 26 he has been working as a professional photojournalist for all major European magazines.

Jorg Muller, Germany
Muller was born in Cologne, Germany. He studied photo-design in Dortmund from 1985 to 1991. Since then, he has been a freelance photographer, and his work has appeared in *Stern, Der Spiegel,* and *Sport.*

Trent Nelson, USA
Nelson is a staff photographer for the *Salt Lake Tribune* who has won numerous photography awards.

Andy Levin

Prayers of the faithful sent by email cover the grave of Rebbe Menacham Schneerson, leader of a Jewish sect. (p. 182)

Grupo Desea

The Zapatista rebels have a secret weapon—and it's the Internet. (p. 204)

Jeremy Nicholl, Russia
Nicholl started his career working as a freelance press photographer in 1981. In 1986 he helped launch a new daily British national newspaper, *The Independent.* Since 1990 he has photographed throughout the former Soviet Union. In 1995 his photographs of the destruction caused by the Russian military assault on Grozny, Chechnya, were shown at the Perpignan Festival of Photojournalism. He is currently working on a book of his photographs of Russia.

Gary O'Brien, USA
O'Brien has been a staff photographer at the *Charlotte Observer* since 1988. In 1993 and 1994 he received the North Carolina News Photographers Association Photographer of the Year award.

Tony O'Brien, USA
O'Brien is currently working on assignment for *Life* magazine, taking an intimate look at monastic life. In the past, he has covered the Afghanistan war, a Mt. Everest summit attempt, and the Persian Gulf War, also for *Life* magazine.

Sam Ogden, USA
Science and high-tech photographer Ogden is a native Bostonian. His photographs have been published in most major science magazines. A regular contributor to *Scientific American* and *Science,* he recently completed photographing a book with world-famous pediatrician T. Berry Brazelton.

Randy Olson, USA
Olson is a contract photographer for *National Geographic,* for which he is currently working in the Ozarks on his sixth assignment. Prior to joining *National Geographic,* he was a staff photographer at the *Pittsburgh Press* for seven years. His awards include Newspaper Photographer of the Year, an Alicia Patterson Fellowship for social documentary, and the Robert F. Kennedy award for social documentary.

Sean Openshaw, USA
Openshaw is chief photographer at the *Arizona Daily Sun* in Flagstaff, Arizona. He teaches basic photojournalism at Northern Arizona University.

Ward Perrin, USA
Perrin has worked as a news photographer and photo editor for a number of Canadian newspapers. He has covered the Clinton-Yeltsin summit, the World Cup, the National Hockey League playoffs, and numerous Canadian political events. Perrin currently works as a picture editor and photographer for the *Vancouver Sun.*

Mark Peters, South Africa
Born in Bulawayo, Zimbabwe, Peters began his career as a news photographer on the *Bulawayo Chronicle.* In 1978 he joined South Africa's largest daily newspaper, *The Star.* In 1984 Peters became a contract photographer for *Newsweek.* He has covered major news stories, including the Persian Gulf War and conflicts in Afghanistan, Israel, China, Rwanda, and Somalia. His February 1990 *Newsweek* cover picture was the first of Nelson Mandela as a free man to be transmitted around the world.

David Peterson, USA
Peterson has won two Pulitzer Prizes: one for feature photography in 1987, and another for public service in 1991. He was a NPPA/Nikon Sabbatical grant recipient in 1986, and won the National Press Photographers Association Photographer of the Year award for Region Five from 1978 to 1980.

Dustin Pittman, USA
After studying film, video, and photography at the School of Visual Arts in New York City, Pittman opened his New York studio. An editorial and advertising photographer with a special interest in technique, he is known for incorporating movement and spontaneous energy in all his work. Dustin has a full-service multimedia production studio in New York that handles interactive as well as linear presentations.

Larry Price, USA
Price is currently employed at the *Fort Worth (Texas) Star-Telegram.* Since the beginning of his photography career in 1977, Price has won two Pulitzer Prizes: in 1981 for his coverage of the Liberian coup, and in 1985 for his photographs of Angola and El Salvador. Price's work has also been honored by the Overseas Press Club, the World Press, and the National Press Photographers Association.

Lois Raimondo, Vietnam
Raimondo is chief photographer for the Associated Press in Hanoi, Vietnam. She has published one book: *The Little Lama of Tibet.* In 1988 she was a Pulitzer Prize finalist for her work as an investigative reporter. She has been a teacher, a reporter, and a photographer and has received many awards for her work.

Roger Ressmeyer, USA
An editorial and advertising photographer specializing in space technology and science, Ressmeyer worked full-time as a freelance contributor to *National Geographic.* He now serves as editor in the media development department of Corbis Corporation, Bill Gates' "other" software company. His 1991–92 award-winning global assignment on volcanoes for *National Geographic* has been turned into a CD-ROM called *Volcanoes: Life on the Edge* (Corbis Publishing, 1996).

Mark Richards, USA
Richards has been a freelance photographer for 10 years, working in Burma, Afghanistan, and Haiti. He has won awards from *Communication Arts* and NPPA, and works with *Time, Newsweek,* and *Fortune.*

Rick Rickman, USA
Rickman's work for *National Geographic* and many other clients has taken him around the world photographing major events. He garnered international recognition in 1985 after winning the Pulitzer Prize for news photography. Rickman was a finalist in the W. Eugene Smith Memorial Grant in 1982 and 1984 and has received numerous awards in the national Pictures of the Year competition.

Steve Ringman, USA
Ringman is a photographer for the *Seattle Times.* He is a two-time winner of the National Press Photographers Association Newspaper Photographer of the Year award and a four-time winner of the San Francisco Bay Area Newspaper Photographer of the Year award. In the early 1980s, he pioneered photojournalistic coverage of the AIDS epidemic.

Denise Rocco, USA
A travel, documentary, and fine-art photographer, Rocco was most recently involved in the production of the book and interactive CD-ROM *Passage to Vietnam.* Previously, she received a grant from the Polaroid Corporation to photograph the public-housing developments of Boston. Counter Culture, her documentary project about American diners, has appeared in numerous galleries across the United States.

Ricki Rosen, Israel
Rosen has worked as a photojournalist for 12 years. For the last seven years, she has been based in Israel, where she has followed the Arab-Israeli conflict. Currently, she is working on two book projects: one on Jerusalem, and the other on the immigration to Israel of a half million refugees from the former Soviet Union and Ethiopia.

Manfred Scharnberg, Germany
Scharnberg studied visual communications at the university in Hamburg. After several exhibitions, he is working as a freelancer for several prominent German magazines.

Michael A. Schwarz, USA
Schwarz is a freelance editorial and corporate journalist based in Atlanta. He has received numerous awards from the Pictures of the Year competition and was a winner of the Dag Hammarskjold award for human rights advocacy journalism. He is cochairman of the Atlanta Photojournalism seminar.

Via email with an on-site scientist, these students are learning volumes about one of earth's least-populated continents. (p. 70)

Before going underground, these spelunkers like to surf the Web. (p. 72)

Thomas L. Kelly

Tradition meets technology in Dharamsala, India, where the exiled Dalai Lama is creating his own website. (p. 206)

Peter Stone

Using the Internet, students across the country have created a living map of the monarch butterfly's annual migration. (p. 75)

Arabella Schwarzkopf, Austria/USA
Schwarzkopf was born in Austria and moved to the United States at age 19. She recently graduated from the Rochester Institute of Technology. Schwarzkopf is currently photographing in New York City. Her photograph was selected from the thousands submitted by students to the *24 Hours in Cyberspace* project on February 8, 1996.

Massimo Siragusa, Italy
Siragusa's interests range from the world of the Vatican to the world of politics and society. Now affiliated with Agenzia Contrasto, he began his professional career in 1987. In 1989 his series of photos taken underwater received an honorable mention in the Italian selection of the European Kodak award.

John Sleezer, USA
Sleezer began taking photographs while in high school in Olathe, Kansas. Following his enlistment in the army, Sleezer earned a bachelor's degree in mass communications at Kansas State University. Since graduating in 1985, Sleezer has worked at several newspapers; for the past seven years he has been on staff at the *Kansas City Star*.

Rick Smolan, USA
A former *Time, Life,* and *National Geographic* photographer, Smolan has spent a decade finding ways to place himself and his projects directly in the path of the converging worlds of photography, design, and publishing technology. In 1981 Smolan created the best-selling Day in the Life book series. More than 3 million copies have been sold to date; *A Day in the Life of America* alone was on the *New York Times* best-seller list for over a year, making it the best-selling photographic title in American history. Four of the books have been featured on the covers of *Time* and *Newsweek*.

Tara Sosrowardoyo, Indonesia
Born into a diplomat's family, Sosrowardoyo was raised in various parts of the world. He has made a name for himself as an art director and photographer of record-album covers, and as a still photographer for the Indonesian feature-film industry. He hopes to be able to open a small digital-imaging studio in Jakarta, Indonesia.

Pall Stefansson, Iceland
Stefansson has been a photographer since 1982 and picture editor since 1985 for *Iceland Review*. His photographs have been published in various magazines worldwide. Stefansson has published three books of photographs: *Light* (1988), *Iceland* (1992), and *Panorama* (1996).

Peter Steinhauer, USA
Steinhauer just returned from Hanoi, Vietnam, where he lived since December 1993. He plans to return so he can continue to photograph the Vietnam that is still untouched by Western culture but is quickly disappearing.

Peter Stone, Mexico
Stone covered the famine in Somalia in 1993 and postcoup Estonia in 1992. He joined Black Star in 1991 and covered the breakup of the Soviet Union from the Baltic Republics. In July 1994 he relocated to Mexico, where he does feature, editorial, and corporate work.

James A. Sugar, USA
Sugar worked as a full-time contract photographer for *National Geographic* from 1969 to 1992 and has taught at photographic workshops nationwide. Among his many awards are the National Press Photographers Association Magazine Photographer of the Year in 1978, first place in nature photography from World Press in 1986, and first place in pictorial in the 1991 White House Press Photographers Association competition.

Dick Swanson, USA
Swanson's work is included in the Museum of Modern Art's permanent collection. In 1995 the Center for American History at the University of Texas, Austin, asked for Swanson's body of work dating back to 1956—work that covers thousands of assignments from 20 different countries and includes some 100,000 photographs, such as his *Life* magazine work during the Vietnam War. He has received awards from the World Press Photo Foundation, the National Press Photographers Association, and the White House Press Photographers Association.

Bill Swersey, USA
Swersey has been a photojournalist since graduating from Boston University in 1984. After freelancing in Boston and New York City, he joined Gamma-Liaison in 1989. In 1991 he became Moscow correspondent for the agency. Swersey organized Interfoto, the first international photojournalism festival in Russia.

Stuart Tannehill, USA
A 1994 graduate of Ohio University, Tannehill attended the 1995 Eddie Adams workshop. He is a staff photographer for the *Florida Times-Union* in Jacksonville.

Patrick Tehan, USA
Tehan is a staff photographer at the *San Jose Mercury News*. He was a runner-up in the 1992 Newspaper Photographer of the Year award.

Scott Thode, USA
Thode's work has been exhibited at the Visa Pour L'image photo festival in Perpignan, France; in the Electric Blanket AIDS Project; at the Colonnade Gallery in Washington, D.C.; and at the P.S. 122 Gallery in New York City. Scott lives in New York City.

Joe Traver, USA
Traver recently concluded his term as the 38th president of the National Press Photographers Association, the first freelance photographer to be elected to the post. He has been nominated for a Pulitzer Prize, and in 1990 he was the National Football League Photographer of the Year.

Alexander Tsiaras, USA
Tsiaras' interests have encompassed photography, writing, painting, architecture, sculpture, furniture design, and documentary filmmaking. He has been an innovator in creating new ways of producing scientific and medical photography. He has lectured widely, including at the Massachusetts Institute of Technology's Media Lab, with mathematician Stephen Hawking. In 1997 Time Warner will publish his work, Anatomical Travelogue, as a book and CD-ROM, with an excerpt scheduled to appear in *Life* magazine.

Mark van Manen, Canada
Vancouver Sun staff photographer van Manen began working in newspapers at age 17. He first started shooting freelance assignments for the *Sun* while working in the paper's photo lab; in the 18 years since, his assignments have taken him around the world.

David Walberg, USA
Walberg has worked as a freelance photojournalist for 17 years, primarily for *Sports Illustrated* and *Newsweek*. He won first place in the Baseball Hall of Fame photo contest.

Bill Warren, USA
Warren was born in Lafayette, Indiana, and is a graduate of Indiana University's School of Journalism. Since 1988 he has worked as a news photographer for the *Ithaca Journal*. He has traveled and photographed extensively in South Asia, including three trips to Dharamsala, India, to photograph exiled Tibetans for the book *Living Tibet: The Dalai Lama in Dharamsala* (Snow Lion Publications, 1995).

Mark S. Wexler, USA
Wexler has covered such diverse topics as the American South for *National Geographic* and Japanese youth for *Smithsonian*. He won three World Press awards for his work on *A Day in the Life of Japan*.

Darren Whiteside, Cambodia
Whiteside has covered Cambodia on a regular basis since 1991 and has been based in Phnom Penh since 1994. He is currently employed as a stringer for Reuters News Picture Service and is a regular contributor to *Asiaweek* and the *Phnom Penh Post*.

J.H. Yun, Korea
A graduate of the Seoul Institute of the Arts, Yun joined the Associated Press in November 1987; he is now AP's chief photographer in Seoul. His assignments have taken him to much of Asia and have run the gamut from sports and features to civil unrest and natural disasters.

Staff

PROJECT MANAGEMENT

Project Directors
Rick Smolan
Jennifer Erwitt

COO and Technical Director
Tom Melcher

Director of Photography and Assignments
Karen Mullarkey

Vice President, Publicity
Patti Richards

Marketing and Student Underground Coordinator
Gina Privitere

Office Manager
Katya Able

Controller
Rita Dulebohn

Production Coordinator
Corey Hajim

Systems Management
Shane Iseminger

Administrative Assistants
Gina Carfora
Sunny Leigh Woodall

Accounting
Bob Powers,
  *Calegari & Morris,
  Accountants*
Eugene Blumberg

Legal Counsel
Barry Reder,
  *Coblentz, Cahen,
  McCabe & Breyer*
Rick Pappas
Jonathan Hart,
  Dow Lohnes & Albertson

Literary Agent
Bill Gladstone,
  Waterside Productions

Picture Syndication
Eliane Laffont
J.P. Pappis,
  Sygma Photo Agency

Printer
Keiichi Ishikawa
Shintaro Shigemori
Jennifer Groom
Mitsuhiro Tada
Minoru Kamigahira
Yuzo Hasegawa
Akira Matsuura
Fujio Takahashi
  Toppan Printing Co.

BOOK

Art Director and Designer
Lori Barra

Writer
Eileen Matthews Hansen

Preface and Essays
Paul Saffo

Assistant to the Designer
Jennifer Friedman

Photoshop Designers
J. Patrick Forden
Jennifer Melnick

Associate Editor
Beatrice Motamedi

Copy Editor
Pat Soberanis

Book Production
Eric and Jan Martí,
  Command Z

Production Assistants
Shane Iseminger
Erik Mathy

Print Broker
Lithomania, Inc.

Technical Advisors
Russell Preston Brown
Diane Burns
Laura Perry

Project Assignment Editors
Kathy Dalle-Molle
J. Carl Ganter
Jane Gottesman
Dogen Hannah
Acey Harper
Alex Lash
Janice Maloney
Tripp Mikich
Lisa Napoli
Evan Nisselson
Barry Sundermeier
Karen Wickre

Associate Assignment Editors
Paul Andrews
Millané Kang
Sumiko Kurita
Mindy Ran
Beth Rickman
Mark Rykoff
Kaz Tsuchikawa

Project Photo Editors
Vin Alabiso,
  Associated Press
Guy Cooper,
  Newsweek Magazine
Cotton Coulson,
  U.S. News & World Report
Mike Davis,
  Detroit Free Press
Scott T. DeMuesy,
  San Jose Mercury News
Gary Fong,
  San Francisco Chronicle
David Friend,
  Life Magazine
Colin Jacobson,
  Reportage
Michele McNally,
  Fortune Magazine
Eric Meskauskas,
  New York Daily News
Maddy Miller,
  People Magazine
Randy Miller,
  Battle Creek Inquirer
Larry Nighswander,
  *Ohio University, School
  of Visual Communication*
Evan Nisselson
Marcel Saba,
  Saba Press Photos
Mike Smith,
  Detroit Free Press
Dieter Steiner,
  Stern Magazine
Michele Stephenson,
  Time Magazine

Associate Photo Editor
Judith Siviglia

Assistant Photo Editor
Julie Coburn

WEBSITE

Information Architect
Clement Mok

Managing Editor, Live Event Website
Spencer Reiss

Managing Editor, Permanent Website
Cotton Coulson

Web Design Coordinator, Live Event Website
Eric Wilson

Senior Art Director, Permanent Website
J. Patrick Forden

Assistant Managing Editor, Permanent Website
Michael Schumann

Senior Editor, Permanent Website
Barry Owen

Publicity Coordinator
Molly Schaeffer

Publicity Assistants
Jennifer Friedman
Sophie Deprez

Editors
Samir Arora
Maggie Canon
Sam Fuetsch
Don George
Tom Goldstein
Guy Kawasaki
Clement Mok
Spencer Reiss
Michael Rogers
Lillian Svec

Table of Contents Editors
Lori Barra
Russell Preston Brown
Robin Burman
Barry M. Schuler
Thomas K. Walker

Essayists
John Perry Barlow
Stewart Brand
Esther Dyson
Al Gore
Howard Rheingold
Paul Saffo

Writers
Jane Meredith Adams
Barbara Assadi
Vince Bielski
Carol Blaney
Dan Brekke
Cameron Crotty
Cecilia Deck
Mark Durham
Dennis Floss
Mark Frost
Jeff Greenwald
Connie Guglielmo
Eileen Matthews Hansen
Laird Harrison
Paul Hilts
Barbara Jamison
Bruce Koon
Susan LaCroix
Josh Levine
Craig Marine
James A. Martin
Jerry Michalski
Beatrice Motamedi
Terry Mulgannon
Jim Paul

Eric Pfeiffer
Scott Rubin
Curt Sanburn
Brent Schlender
Ken Siegmann
Steve Silberman
Miriam Silver
Belinda Taylor

Chief Copy Editor
Janice Maloney

Copy Editors
Paul Bacon
Jean Williams Brusher
Lorraine Fry
Erica H. Gies
Elizabeth Leahy
Charles J. Lenatti
Pat Soberanis

Text Traffic
Austin Willacy

Mission Control Coordinator
Anne Murray

Logistics Coordinators
James Able
Katya Able
Jennifer Scott

Sponsor Coordinator
Amy Bonetti

Television Consultants
David Avery
Mike Cerre

Production Assistants
Bill Buck
Paul Diamond
Andrew Ettelson
Andrea Ferretti
Alex Fordyce
Eric Fox
Andy Fusso
Jeanne-Marie Jasko
Jonathan King
Tina Loukianoff
Nicole Newham
Rob Penn
Kris Peternie
Desiree Pointer
Deno Prokos
Eric Rosenberg
Joan Rosenberg
Jason Russell
Stacey Schreiber
John David Scott
ElenaTecglen
Natasha Urtiew
Charlie Wagner
Austin Willacy
B.J. Wooten

Systems Integration Director
John Graham

Director of Photo Technologies
Donald Winslow

Photo Technologies Coordinator
Kurt Foss

Associated Press Coordinator
Neal Ulevich

Assistant to the Technical Director
Marc Escobosa

Systems Administration
Dave De Graff
Marc Escobosa
Matt Graham
Phil Hopper

Image Traffic
Julie Coburn
Jerry De Avila
Dave De Graff
Kurt Foss
Scott Henry
Mark Loundy
Evan Nisselson
Jason Russell
Katie Silberman
Judith Siviglia
Neal Ulevich
Kirk Van Druten
Michael Zilber

Photoshop and HTML Programming
Dana Ahlfeldt
Bob Albert
Devon Beisler
Daniel Alan Brown
Brett Butterfield
Matt Carlson
Maren Caruso
George Chen
Julie Coburn
Matthew Cotter
Guillermo Fausto
Sarah Fawcett
J. Patrick Forden
Carl Goldschmidt
Matt Graham
Corey Hajim
Pete Hogg
Shane Iseminger
George Jardine
Louis Lee
Vlad Lyubovny

Magali Mabari
Erik Mathy
Luke McDowell
Ron Neal
Duane Nelson
Philip O'Neil
Bill Owen
David Pearce
Gina Privitere
Doug Rea
Elizabeth Ryan
Michael Schumann
Audrey Shehyn
Judith Siviglia
Erica L. Wilcot
Eric Wilson

Mission Control Technical Support Team
Sal Arora
Samir Arora
John Barry
Shaun Bliss
Anthony Brown
Greg Brown
Marie Brown
Bill Burke
Mike Carrier
Patricia Chalupa
Winston Chin
Bill Coppens
Christina Cory
Steve Davis
Moneka Dean
Carrie Dillon
Mike Douglas
Jacque Eidson
Ray Felton
Mike Freame
Anil Gadre
Tom Gaffney
Steve Gibson
Michele Gould
Jennifer Graham
Chris Haaga
Barb Hardaway
Greg Herring
Burt Heymanson
Derek Hill
Phil Hopper
Agnes Imregh
Cindy Iwamura
Diana Jerolimov
Zak Jones
Surya Josula
Marc Kirschner
David Kleinberg
Teresa Lau
Leiann Lee
Noel Lopez
David Marsyla
Court Mast
Carl Meske
Ren Moore

Kristine O'Berry
George Paolini
Bill Ray
Joe Roebuck
Kevin Roebuck
Kathy Ryan
Steve Sabram
Stephanie Sacks
Russ Sage
Marina Salume
Hassan Schroeder
Dave Segleau
Susan Seigal
Maureen Shea
Martin Siegmenthaler
Shane Sigler
Phil Smyth
Scott Spelbring
Judy Tarabini
John Taylor
Mark Tolliver
Toshiharu Tsuji
Martin Venezky
Katherine Webster
Michelle Wilcox
Linda Witkop
Tony Wittry
Jeff Yau
Dale Yoakam
Jeff Zank
Vic Zauderer
Laura Zung

Audio Director
Pat Flynn

Audio Coordinator
J. Carl Ganter

Audio Interviewers
Isabel Alegria
Alex Bennett
John Burks
Rachel Gotbaum
Harry Lin
Curt Sanburn
Eileen Wray McCann

Field Audio Reporters
Virginia Biggar
Sarah Chayes
Mandalit Del Barco
Gene Endres
Beth Fertig
Pat Ford
Rachel Gotbaum
Linda Gradstein
John Gregory
John Hauber
Gene Bryan Johnson
Ian Jowitt
Lauri Neff
Belamy Pailthorp
Michael Richards
Mark Roberts

Andrew Robins
Tara Siler
Joe Smith
Robert Smith
Michael Ura
Tanya Van Valkenburg
Laura Ziegler
Brian Zumhagen

Audio Technical Engineer
Dan Augustine

Audio Technicians
Mark Ely
Vance Gallaway
David J. Gray
Gary Hall
Jonathan Hoffberg
Lisa Jaime
Richard Levitt
Jim Moorer
Sean Penn

Digital Imaging
David Alexander
Drew Glickman
Bob Goldstein
Mario Gomez
Kim Kapin
David Salinas

Telecommunications Coordinator
William McCauley

Contest Coordinator
Laura Zung

Infographic Designer
Nigel Holmes

Logo Animation
Jacob Trollbeck,
    R/Greenberg Associates

Interns
John Black
James Cheng
Chien-min Chung
Adam Doti
Elaine Fellenbaum
Apolinar Fonseca
Steve Fujimoto
Susie Kameny
Christine L. Mirigian
Torrey Nommesen

QUE®/Macmillan Computer Publishing
Roland Elgey
Stacy Hiquett
Jeff Valler
Lynn Zingraf
Barry Pruett

Friends and Advisors

We would like to thank the thousands of individuals worldwide whose invaluable assistance made this project possible. Without their unwaivering commitment, skill, and enthusiasm, these pages would be blank.

Alexandra Able
Moriko & Norika Adachi
John Adams
Mike Adams
Noah Adams
Helene Adkin
Dan Adler
Shahidul Alam
Rhoda & Ira Albom
Geoff Alderman
Pam Alexander
John Alfano
John Allen
Paul Allen
Monica Almeida
Stewart Alsop
Ralph Alswang
John Altberg
Sally Aman
Paul Ambrose
Hector Amezquita
Philip Anast
Craig Anderson
Eric C. Anderson
Erik Anderson
Jane Anderson
Terry Anderson
Andrea, Matteo &
   Maddalena
Marc Andreessen
Robert Andrews
Joseph Ansanelli
Cornellio Antonio
Nancy Appleby
Michael Apted
Efi Arazi
Amy Arnold
Ed Arnold
Johanna Arnold
Stephen Arnold
Burt Arnowitz
Sal Arora
Samir Arora
Karen Arthur
Rea Ashley
Rebecca Astorga
Bill & Susan Atkinson
David Auch
Dan Augustine
Anette Ayala
Eddie Babcock
Larry Baca
Eric Bachman
Mike Backes
Dan Backus
Jeff Baehr
Jennifer Baily
Ron Baird
Tim Bajarin
David Baker
Deborah Baker
John Baker
Sheldon Baker
Stephen Baker
Alan Baldwin
Steve Balkin
Chris Balla
Iskra Banova
Rogers Bar
Bob Barbour

Katherine Barcos
Michael Barker
Angus Barnes
Judy Barnett
Andrew & Lissa Barnum
Ed & Rena Barnum
Fiona Baron
Allan Barr
Fran, Tom, &
   Christine Barra
Lucille & Thomas Barra
Peter Barrett
Lisa Barsotti
Sandra Bateman
Bill Bates
Randy Battat
Mary K. Bauman
Jane Bay
Chip Bayers
Ron Beaumont
Rudy Becks
Jim Beiersdorf
David Beigie
Herrman Bellinghausen
Keith Bellows
Annie Griffith Belt
Paul Benati
Esther Benenson
Reed Benet
Thomas Bennett
Paul Benoit
Tom Bentkowski
P.F. Bentley
Randi Benton
Patricia Bentson
Jocelyne Benzakin
Roger Berdam
Mike Berger
Gussie Bergerman
George Berhitoe
William Berkman
David Berkowitz
Christine Berman
Ruth & Harris Berman
Richard Bernstein
Joe Bernui
Eric Berryman
Mark Bersheni
David Best
Tom Bettag
Sanjay Bhalala
Carole Bidnick
Nick Billow
Roger Birnbaum
Lori Birtley
Mike Blake
Gail Blumberg
Larry Bobroski
Janneke Bogyo
Jude Bolan
Floris de Bonneville
Mike Borsetti
Alexandra Bost
Pierce & Donna Bounds
Tim Bouwer
Kathy Bower
Laverne Boyd
Father Boyle
Jessica Brackman
Heather Bradley

Richard Bradley
Willie Bradley
Holly Brady
Paul Brainerd
Cabell Brand
Jim Breyer
Marshall & Nina Brickman
Sue Brisk
John Brockman
Denise Brosseau
Daniel Brown
David Brown
Edward Espe Brown
Luther Brown
Margot Brown
Peter T. Brown
Rick Brown
Wendy Buchberg
Mimi & Peter Buckley
Hal Buell
Emma Bufton
Jane Bunch
Al & Dawn Bunetta
David Bunnell
Phil Burfurd
Rudy Burger
Ann Burgraff
Margaret Burk
Bill Burke
K.B. Burke
David & Iris Burnett
Arnold Burns
Red Burns
Darryl Bush
Kathy Bushkin
Patrick Butler
Robert Olin Butler
Stephanie Calabrese
Ben Calica
Sean Callahan
Reid Callanan
Nicholas & Yukine Callaway
Elsa Cameron
Jane Cameron
Sheila Cameron
Woody Camp
Bill Campbell
Dan Campi
Kevin Cancilla
Jim Cansella
Marc & Devorah Canter
Maria Cantowell
Cornell Capa
Steve Capps
Roger Caras
Ken & Janet Carbone
Georges Cardona
Monte Carlos
Doug Carlson
Tom Carmichael
Sean Carmody
Oscar Carrion
Lisa Carroccio
John Mack Carter
Todd Carter
Guenther Cartwright
Veronica Cartwright
Denise Caruso
Frank Casanova
Jane & Ed Case
Steve Case
Ted Casey
Phil Casini
Marguerita Castanera
Dr. Frank Catchpool
Barbara Cavalier
Linda Cernik-Price
Gina Cerre
Mr. Chandra

Stephen Chao
Howard & Jeanette
   Chapnick
Sergio Charlab
Brad Chase
Steve Chernoff
Mary Chin
Lyn Chitow
Will Cho
Harriett Choice
Vickram Chrishna
Cindi Christie
Albert Chu
Laurence Chu
Ivan Chung
Bob Ciano
Vincent Cimino
Rose Ann Cimino-Scott
Jess & Rhoda Claman
Andy Clark
Jim Clark
Linda Clark
Rich Clarkson
Michael Clasen
Danny Clay
Lisa Cleary
Harry Cleaver
Josephine & Margaret Clift
Shane & Megan Clift
Craig Cline
John Coate
Jodi Cobb
Luanne Cohen
James Coleman
Jennifer Coley
Budd Colligan
John Collins
Terry Collins
S. Colombatto
John Colston
Jimmy Colton
Don Conklin
Nellie Connors
Michael Conti
Robert Conway
Andrea Cook
Bob Cook
Rob & Mary Anne Cook
Scott Cook
Julia Coppersmith
Joel Copple
Jack & Helen Corn
Matt Costello
Sheila Costello
Cate Cowan
Ray Cox
Patrick Coyne
Don Crabb
Kim Criswell
Robert Croog, Esq.
Karen Cross
Mark Crumpacker
John Cunin
Andy Cunningham
Richard Cure
Paul Curtis
Richard Curtis
Heidi Cuttler
Eric Dahlinger
Yogan Dalal
Deputy Dorothy Daley
Marie D'Amico
Hidetoshi Danjo
Bruce Danzer
Robyn Davidson
Diane Davis
Jan Davis
Anne Day
Ed Deal

Keith Deaven
Mark Decker
Cliff Deeds
Eddie DeJesus
Susan de la Cruz
Mike Demers
Ray & Barbara DeMoulin
Lee Denny
Alma Derricks
Peter & Randall deSeve
Giuseppe de Vincentis
Djibirl Diallo
Raul Diaz
Ron Dickson
Nick Didlick
Charles Dilworth
Dennis Dimick
Walter Dods
John Doerr
Michael Dolbec
Claire Donahue
Sheila Donnelly
Joel Donnet
Michael Donovan
Bob Doris
David & Ann Doubilet
Charlie Dow
Lisa Downey
Maria Doyle
Arnold Drapkin
Fred Dresner
Gene & Gayle Driskell
Tony Driskell
Hugh Dubberly
Hank Duderstadt
Patty DuFresne
Dave Duggal
John Duhring
Ken & Pam Duncan
Bill Dunn
John & Eileen Dunn
John Durniak
Deb Dvir
Mary Dawn Earley
LaWonda Eastwood
Fred Ebrahimi
Nicy Echavez
Alex Edelstein
Phillip Edney
Elyssa Edwards
Owen & Regine Edwards
Barbara Egan
Jody Ehlers
Ginny Ehrlich
Dan Eilers
Lee Eisenberg
Mark Ely
Michela English
Brian Erickson
Amy Erwitt
David, Sheri, Erik, &
   C.J. Erwitt
Ellen Erwitt
Elliott Erwitt
Sasha Erwitt
Gerry Esposito
Dale Ester
Steve Ettlinger
Gordon Eubanks
John & Yonge Evans
Michael Evans
Tim Evard
Jeffrey J. Ewing
John Faherty
David Fanning
Richard Farana
Daniel & Elinore Farber
Steve Farrell
Edie Farwell

Amy Faulkner
Liz Faulkner
Henry Feinberg
Harlan Felt
Bran Ferren
John Files
Janine Firpo
Allen Fischer
Sydney Fisher
Michael Fitzpatrick
Randy Fleming
Barb Golle Fleming
Vivienne Flesher
Penny Foldenauer
Ben Fong-Torres
Rick Ford
Bob Forst
Hamish Forsythe
Paul Foschino
Jon Fox
Lauren Fox
Marty Fox
Theresea Francis
Christa & Florentina
   Frangiamore
Chris Frescholtz
Wendy Friedman
Tom Fristoe
Elizabeth Frost
Mark Frost
Fred Fuchs
Mami Fujii
Joe Fuller
Becky Fuson
Art Gable
Peter Gabriel
Gary Gach
John Gaffney
Gordon Gallagher
Tracy Gallagher
David Gang
Stuart Gannes
Marvin & Leslie Gans
Lisa Gansky
Laurine Garaude
Sam Garcia
Terry Garnett
Gary Garriott
Chris Garvey
Jean Louis Gassee
Sandra Gault
Bruce Gee
Scott Geffert
Pamela Geismar
Noreen Geistle
Elyse Genuth
Stefanos Georgantis
Luan Giannone
Greg Gibson
Jimmy Gichui
Miles Gilburn
Tom & Peg Gildersleeve
Bob Gilka
Brendan Gill
Greg Gilles
Julia Gillet
Shannon Gilligan
Alexis Girard
Paul Giurata
Rob Glaser
Jennifer Glass
Joe Glass
Neil Glassman
Steve Glenn
Ira Glick
David Glickman
Drew Glickman
Vicky Godbey
David Godine

Diego Goldberg
Nat & Marilyn Goldhaber
David Goldman
Lisa Goldman
Howard Goldstein
Suzanne Goldstein
Sue Goldy
Anastasio Gomes
Rolando Gomes
Ed Gomez
Beth Gonzales
Isidro Gonzalez
Amanda Goodenough
Danny Goodman
Ford Goodman
Roberta Goodman
Carter Goodrich
Jim Gordon
Mark Gorenberg
Joel Gottler
Flo & Arthur Grace
Carol Graebner
John Grant
Brian Grazer
Jessica Green
Nancye Green
Susan Greenbaum
Martin & Liz Greenberger
Rodney Greenblat
George Greenfield
Jeff Greenwald
Mick Greenwood
Steve Gregory
Bill Gross
Snorri Gudjónsson
Hilmar Thor
   Gudmundsson
Alan Gunshure
Kendall Guthrie
Ken Haase
Christine Haenn
Ed & Barbara Hajim
Justin Hall
Lynn Hamb
Robert Hamilton
Herbie Hancock
Jody Hansen
Lisbet & Mac Hansen
Michael Hanson
John Harcourt
Gary Hare
Cheri Hariri
Vaughn Harring
Rosa Harrington
Jay Harris
Nick & Jane Harris
Patricia Hartigan
Buzz Hartshorn
Pieter Hartsook
Adnan Hassan
David Hathaway
Larry Hatlett
Selma Hauser
Vicki Hawkins
Steve Hayden
David Hazlett
Will Hearst
Francois Hebel
Jenny Hedges
Mark Brooks Hedstrom
Kate Heery
Christie Heffner
Ginny Heinlein
Hugh Hempel
Scott Henry
Jenelle Hermann
John Hermes
Rosa Herrington
Rob Herron

Carolyn Herter
Andy Hertzfeld
Eric Herzog
Carl Hewitt
Martine Heyer
Doug Hickey
Terry Hicks
James Higa
Scott Highton
Daniel Hill
John Hill
Rowland & Sue Hill
Dale Hinkson
Shuly Hirsch
Noël Hirst
Tom Hoehn
Sam Hoffman
Randy Hogue
Matt Holland
Anneliese Hollman
Nigel & Erin Holmes
Kim Honda
Nancy Hooff
Will Hopkins
Sean & Anna Hopper
Pavel Horejsi
Melissa Horn
John Houser
David Howard
Ron Howard
Anita Howe-Waxman
Thomas Hsieh
Lin Hsin Hsin
Michael Hudes
John Huey
Drew Huffman
David Hughes
Adrienne Humphrey
Liam Hunt
Bradley Husick
Lindsey & Paul Iacovino
Tsyoshi Inaba
Kenneth Irby
Christopher Ireland
Chuck & Carol Isaacs
Walter Isaacson
Diane Iselin
Andrea Israel
Joichi Ito
Vern & Pigeon Iuppa
Pico Iyer
Naomi Izakura
Eran Jachdav
Charlie Jackson
Rita Jacobs
Tom Jacobs
Amy Janello
Glen Janssens
Ken Jarecke
Natalie Jenkins
Peter Jennings
Bill Jesse
Christy Jewell
Rick Jiloty
James Joaquin
Steve Jobs
Eggert Jóhannesson
Judith & Richard
   Johnson-Marsano
Amanda & Greg Jones
Brennon Jones
Eleanor Jones
Margaret Jones
Michael Jones
Randy Jones
Reese Jones
Petr Josek
Hal Josephson
Cecil Juanarena &

Kate Yuschenkoff
Brian Judah
Steve Kahng
Robert Kaiser
Thomas Kalil
Hiroaki Kanehara
Millane Kang
Cheryl Kann
Dr. John Kao
Kim Kapin
Rick Kaplan
Mitchell Kapor
Pierre Karaan
Susan Kare
Jessica Kass
Andrew Katz
Bruce Katz
Roberta Katz
Michael Kaufman
Beth Kawasaki
Alan Kay
Father Alfred Keane
Col. John "Jack" Kehoe
Jay Kelbley
Sherri Kellman
Thomas Keneally
Benita Kenn
Peter Kennard
Peter Kennedy
Tom Kennedy
David Kennerly
Dan Kern
John Kernan
Michael Kerwin
Andrew Kessler
Gil Keltelas
Kristin Keyes
Sat Tara Khalsa
Vinod Khosla
Brad Kibbel
Greg Kiernan
Peggy Kilburn
Brenda Kincade
John King
Brad Kirkpatrick
Judy Kirkpatrick
Robert Kirschenbaum
Daphne Kis
Victor Kitpentee
Michael & Veronica
   Kleeman
Harlan & Liz Kleiman
Joyce Klein
Neal Klein
Evie Kling
Tim Kness
Peter Knight
Shigeo Kogure
Jim Kohlenberger
Halldór Kolbeins
Paul Koontz
Péter Korniss
Leslie Kossoff
Kristin Kovacic
Karen Kozak
Peggy Kozy
Capt. Charles M. Kraft, Jr.
Judith Krantz
Tony Krantz
Kai Kraus
Kevin Krejci
Jill Krementz
Jeff Kriendler
Chris Kryzan
John & Vicki Kryzanowski
Katsuyasu Kubota
Nadya Kulakova
John Kunze
Jim Kuon

Sumiko Kurita
Sherman Kwok
Wei-Tai Kwok
Eliane Laffont
Stephanie Laffont
Andrew Laine
Michele Laird
Susan Lake
Phil Lam
Bob Lambert
Sonia Land
Patricia Landis
Richard Landry
Bill Lane
Judy Lang
Jaron Lanier
Alexandra LaNoue
Kristi Larsen
Todd Lash
Jen Latham
Brenda Laurel
Kelly Lavigne
David Lawrence
Jim Leal
John Leddy
Carole Lee
Elnora Lee
Paul Lefebvre
Alan Lefkof
John Lent
Kyle Leonhardt
Rick LePage
Ken Lerer
Rich Levandov
Hugh Levin
Martin Levin
Mel Levine
Larry Levitsky
Bob Levitus
Steve Levy
Daniel & Susan Lewin
Andrew Lewis
Barry Lewis
Howard Lewis & Rachel Hynd
Leo Lewis
Peter Lewis
Jed Lewison
David Liddle
Ken Lien
Jessica Lifland
Andy Lilien
Leticia Limon
Sondhi Limthongkul
Gail Lione
Carmen Lira
Christopher Lloyd
Robert Lockhart
John Loengard
Don Logan
Arsenio Lopez
Richard LoPinto
Doreen Lorenzo
Ellie Louise
Robyn Low
Ming Lu
Gerd Ludwig
Noelani Luke
Paul Lundahl
Tim Lundeen
Bob Lundquist
David Lyman
Kelly Lyon
Michael Mace
Doug Mackenzie
Peter Mackey
Mark Maden
David Madison
Nancy Madlin
Diedre Madsen

Michael & Michelle
   Magnus
Marina Mahathir
Paul Mahon
John Mahr
John Maier
Josh Mailman
Jay & L.A. Maisel
Nakazono Makoto
Michael Malaga
Carl Malamud
Roger Malina
Laura Malone
Alfred Mandel
Tom Mangelsen
Liddy Manson
Al Manzello
Subcomandante Marcos
Bruce Margetich
Joel Margoles
Gerald Margolis
Mary Ellen Mark
John Markoff
Harry Marks
Van Maroevich
Nora & Emma Martí
Nicole Martin
Sherron Martinez
Rick Marucci
Julie Mason
Davis Masten
Richard Masur
Lucienne & Richard
   Matthews
David Maung
Johnny Maung
C.J. Maupin
Margaret Maupin
Holly Maxon
Christine Maxwell
Tanya Mazorowski
Mike & Martha Mazzaschi
Paul McAfee
Stewart McBride
Laurie McClean
Caitlin McClure
Mike McConnell
David McCool
Brendan McDermid
Nion McEvoy
Debbie McFadden
Steve McGeady
Katie McGrath
Pam McGraw
MaryAnn McGregor
John McKay
Shawn McKee
Liz Perle McKenna
Regis McKenna
Gary McKinnis
Laurie McLean
Mike McMahon
Meghan McNabb
Ardsley McNeilly
Kevin McVea
Meg McVey
Jack McWilliams
Mike Medavoy
Mary Meeker
Dilip Mehta
Melissa Meiris
Bill Melcher
Charles Melcher
Jim Melcher
Miranda Melcher
Samantha Melcher
Su Melcher
Adrian Mello
Kirsty Melville

Chris Mende
Lisa Mendoza
Brita Meng
Tereza Menuez
Charlie Mervus
Hilary Meserole
Joyce Meskis
Bill Messing
Jane Metcalf
Robert Metcalfe
David Metz
John Metzger
Bryan Meyers
Sharon Middendorf
Carl Middlehurst
Jim Miho
Anne Miller
Bob Miller
Jay Miller
Michael Miller
Nicole Miller
Rand & Robyn Miller
Tom Miller
Pam Miracle
Andy Mitchell
Fred Mitchell
John W. Mitchell
John Hollenbeck
   Moczygemba
Maria Monteverde
Bradley Montgomery
Kathleen Moody
Robin Moody
Dr. James E. Moon
Amy Moore
John Moore
Michael Moore
Paula Moore
Ed Moose
Carol Moran
Kathleen Moran
Josh Morgan
Ray Morgan
Marney Morris
Ann Moscicki
Jennifer Moses
Nora & Hugh Moss
Robin & Boots Moyer
Beatrice Mullarkey
Jon Mumper
Kate Myers
Yuji Nagasawa
Hank Nagashima
Emiko Nagayama
David Nagel
Tom Nagorski
Vick Nakamura
Graham Nash
Hilary Nation
Wayne Neale
Eric Nee
David Needle
David Beffa Negrini
Nicholas Negroponte
Peter & Judy Nelson
Gracia Neri
Paul Netikosol
Paul Newis
Bill Newlin
Kim Nguyen
Trish Nicholas
Donna Nicoletti
Abigail Niesus
Gerri Nietzel
Kathy Nilles
Teiichi Nishioka
Wayne Niskala
Chris Noble
Kathy Noesen

Allen Noren
Don Norman
Glenn Norris
Amanda North
Chuck & Shirley Novak
Aleksey Novicov
Yukio Oba
Marianna O'Brien
Patty O'Brien
G.M. O'Connell
Rory O'Connor
Bernard Ohanian
Frank Ohlin
Ingibjorg Olafsdottir
Karen Olcott
Arthur Ollman
Jennifer Olmholt
Michael Olmstead
Lennox Ong
Hirota Ooka
Dean Ornish
Cathy O'Rourke
Alan Orso
Raul Ortega
Will Osborne III
Larry O'Shaunesy
Dan O'Shea
Dan Oshima
Willie Osterman
Gene Ostroff
Mark Ouimet
Michael Ovitz
John Owen
Mark Pachter
Debra Pagan
Mike Pagano
Joshua Mann Pailet
Bill Pakela
Pete Palermo
Rusty Pallas
Heidi Palmer
John Palmer
Richard Paoli
J.P. Pappis
Andy Park
Katherine Parker
Amy Woodward Parrish
Tim Parrish
Carole & George Paton
Dick Patterson
Shawn Pattison
Susannah Patton
Daniel Paul
Kirk Paulsen
Walter Paulsen
Thom Paulson
George Paxenos
Carlos Payan
William Porter Payne
Lee Pazer
Stephen & Kim mai Pearce
Norman Pearlstine
Hilary Peck
LaVon Peck
Jonathan Peizer
Shana Penn
Jason Pentecost
Amy Penticoff
Gabe Perle
Jennifer Persson
David Pescovitz
Carol Peters
Linda Lamb & Rich Peters
Tom Peters
Brent Peterson
Holly Peterson
Ken Phan
Patricia Phelan
John & Janet Pierson

Barbara Pillsbury
Alessandro Piol
Elizabeth Pisani
Carl & Ruth Pite
Jon & Catrine Pite
Stephen Pite
Bill Pitlovany
Sierra Pittman
Skylar Pittman
John Place
Frank Plaster
Catherine Pledge
Robert Pledge
Ronald Pledge
David Plotnikoff
Harry Polatsek
Len Polisar
Elizabeth Pope
Jan Porter
Jo Candido Portinari
Penny Post
Greg Posten
Paige Powell
Marissa Privitere
Thomas M. Privitere
Thomas V. Privitere
Natasha & Jeff Pruss
Deepak Puri
John Quist
Robert Rabkin
Peter Rack
Mitch Radcliff
Jeneanne Rae
Steve Rahe
Jesus Ramires
Michael Rand
Damon Rando
Nathan Rapheld
Phil Rappaport
Patty Rattanavichai
Peter Rattray
Ronda Rattray
Nora Rawlinson
Ron Reams
Bob Reed
Eli Reed
Pamela Reed
Susan Reich
Amy Rennert
Michael Rex
Nick Rhodes
Rachel Ricafrente
Doug Rice
Tracy Rice
Robin Richards
Robert Richman
Thomas P. Rielly
Susan Riker
Bill Rinehart
Renee Risch
Barbara Roberts
Eric Roberts
Jeffrey Roberts
Noel Roberts
Ty Roberts
Debbie Donnelly &
    Justin Robinson
Sally Robson
Anita Roddick
Soldie Rojo
Bill Rollinson
Ronn Ronck
David Rose
Judd Rose
Dave Roselle
Joan Rosenberg
Matt Ross
Louis Rossetto
Ellie Louise Rossiter

Joe Roth
Marvin Rothamn
Galen & Barbara Rowell
Ted Rozolis
Mike Ruby
Sandy Rudloff
John Rugo
Joe Runde
Dean Rutz
Carole Ruwart
Bob Ryan
Kevin Ryan
Margaret Ryan
Tom & Darlene Ryder
Mark Rykoff
Paul & Jennifer Saffo
Nola Safro
Liz Saint John
Masaaki Sakata
Josep Saldana
Lelia & Sebastiao Salgado
David Salinas
Arthur Salsfass
Vieri & Rebecca Salvadori
Thubten Samdup
Marianne Samenko
Will & Marta Sanburn
Jared Sandberg
H. Lockwood Sanders
Tom Santos
J.P. Sartre
Amy Satran
Mary Sauer
Scott Sawry
Barb Sayers
Murray & Jenny Sayle
Dick Schaap
Sonya Schaefer
Steve Schaffer
Steve Schaffren
David Schargel
Aaron Schindler
Gabriele Schindler
D'Anne Schjerning
Mark Schlichting
Eric Schmidt
Jennifer Schmidt
Jeff Schon
Steve Schreck
Barry Schuler
Duane Schulz
Adrienne Schure
Mark Schurman
James Schwabe
David Schwartz
John P. Schweitzer
Julie Schwerin
Doug Scott
Marc Scott
Pat & Karen Scott
Robert E. Scott
Stacey Scott
Robert Scypinski
Richard Seaman
Andrey Sebrant
Scott Sedlik
Lisa See
Paula Seibel
Carol Weiss Seidman
Tom Sellars
Jonathan Seybold
Ann Jennings Shackelford
Dr. Ajit Shah
Neil & Karen Shakery
Ira Shapiro
Maryanne Sharp
Marni Sharr
David Sheff
Kathleen Shehan

Aliza Sherman
Stephanie Sherman
Makota Shimizu
Tsutomo Shimomura
Maki Shinohara
Vicki Shipkovitz
Stephanie Shoemaker
Andrew Shore
Daniel Shoskes, MD
Greg & Cindy Shove
Anu Shukla
Julie Shumskaya
Dave Siegel
Shane Sigler
Rosanne Siino
Madhulika Sikkam
Walter Silva
Terry Silveira
Dwight Silverman
Aaron Singer
Andrew Singer
Bob Siroka
Alison Siu
Richard Skeie
Don Skipton
Bob Skubic
Mike Slade
Aviva Slessin
John Sloss
Brian Smiga
Bill Smith
Brad Smith
Brian Smith
Buford Smith
Charlie Smith
Corey Smith
Gina Smith
Jeanette Smith
Jeffrey Smith
Kim Smith
Martin Cruz Smith
Mary Smith
Megan Smith
Rick Smith
Rodney Smith
Leslie Smolan
Marvin & Gloria Smolan
Reed & Lilly Smolan
Sandy Smolan
Savannah Smolan
Jim Sniffen
Robert E. Snodgrass
Joy & Marty Solomon
Peter Songpon
Scott Sowry
Michele Spane
Joe & Maura Sparks
Mike Spataro
Ed Spencer
Lisa Spivey
Alan Spoon
Suzanne Sprague
Bob Spring
Ahn Stack
Sally Stapleton
Ron Star
Aleen Stein
Scott Stein
Sydney Stein
Henry Steiner
Howard Steinman
Greg Steltenpohl
Chris Stevenson
Andy Stewart
Lisa Stimmel
Tamara Stock
Court Stockton
Jim Stockton
Cliff Stoll

Greg Stone
Julie Stone
Linda Stone
Nancy Stone
Oliver Stone
Dave Strohm
Hal Stucker
Steve Stücky
Dr. Michael Stuewe
Tom Suitor
Jim Sullivan
Tony Sun
Bob Surman
Peter Sutch
Linda Sutherland
Jon Svenson
Dick & Germaine Swanson
James Swartz
Greg Swayne
Steve Sweitzer
David Swift
Martin Swig
Rick Swig
Magdi & Janos Szaktilla
Jeremy Tachau
Rob Taggart
Drew Takahashi
Hidehisa Takahashi
Yuuichi Takanami
Masaya Takemori
Nan Talese
Jay Tannenbaum
Laura Tarrish
Ed Taylor
Michael Tchao
Armen Ter-Minasian
Mike Tharp
Paul Theroux
Kathy Thomas
Frank Thomasson
Christine Thompson
Carol & Chris Thomsen
Charles & Cindy
    Tillinghast III
James Tillinghast
Ruthanne Tim-Siedhoff
Alexandria Todd
Shumpei Tohohuku
Ellen Tolmie
Tomasz Tomaszewski
Shuuhei Tomita
Steve Tomlin
Enzo Torresi
Derek Torrey
Jay Townsend
Lisa Trail
Tom Troung
Kaz Tsuchikawa
Sergey Tsumbalenko
Karen Tucker
Rusty Tucker
Mary Turnbull
Susan Twain
David Umansky
Eric & Nina Utne
Louise Valesquez
Vicki Vance
Michael van der Kieft
Steve VanDuser
Della Van Heyst
Vea Van Kessel
Mimi Van Son
Ignacio Vasallo
Jim Vastola
Paul Villadoid
Jean Villanueva
Alberto Vitali
Janet Vito
Leigh & Laurie Wachter

Susan Wadlington
Charlotte Walker
Jim Wallace
Chip Walters
Susan Walters
Kevin Wandryk
Min Wang
Tim Ware
Bill & Alyssa Warner
Marva Warnock
Marc Warren
Larry Wash
Al Waxman
Chadia Webb
Franki Webster
Margorie Week
William Wegman
Joshua Weisberg
Jeffrey Weiss
Andrew Welch
Lisa Wellman
Albert Wen
Jeffrey West
Rebecca Wetzel
Kathleen Whalen
Megan Wheeler
Dorothy Whitaker
James Wiebe
Sherri Wigger
John Wilczak
Alana Wilding
Maria Wilhelm
Harry Wilker
Barbara Lee Williams
Marsha & Robin Williams
Preston Williams
Elizabeth Willis
Mick Wilson
Gordon Wiltsie
Ann Winblad
Matt & Julie Winokur
Rylan Winslow
Dale Winson
Frankie Winter
Charlie Winton
Michael Witlin
David Wolf
Gary Wolf
Paul Wolf
Curtis Wong
David Wong
Frank Wong
Henry Wong
Michael Wong
Emily Woods
Peter Workman
Sam & Max Worrin
Simon Worrin
Steve Wozniak
Ching Wu
Reven Wurman
Richard Saul Wurman
Dr. John Wynn-Jones
Jerry Yang
Tom Yellin
Magdalena Yesil
Gary Young
Jonathan Young
Yvonne Young
Ann Yow
Mike Zacchino
Robbin Zeff
Brandy Zellers
Mike Zerby
Mel & Pat Ziegler
Moses Znaimer
Emil Zola
Nina Zolt

Platinum Sponsors

 Kodak is the world's leader in imaging and is now extending its traditional strengths in film photography to innovative digital photography products. For *24 Hours in Cyberspace*, Kodak provided all film and processing; Kodak Digital Science tools such as digital cameras, scanners, and printers; Kodak Photo CD technology; and photography publishing expertise. **www.kodak.com**

 Sun coined the phrase "the network is the computer," and that early vision has translated into Sun's Internet leadership today. For *24 Hours in Cyberspace*, Sun provided the servers, storage, and workstations for Mission Control, Internet security expertise, Java programming creativity, and systems integration services. **www.sun.com**

Adobe Adobe Systems, the leader in digital publishing tools, offers a complete line of authoring tools, design tools, and management software for Internet publishing. For *24 Hours in Cyberspace*, Adobe provided graphics, publishing, and Internet solutions, including Adobe Acrobat, Adobe PageMill, and Adobe Photoshop for the websites; Adobe PageMaker and Adobe Illustrator for the book; and Adobe Premiere and Adobe After Effects for the CD-ROM. **www.adobe.com**

Gold Sponsors

 America Online is the world's leading online service, with more than 6 million members. For *24 Hours in Cyberspace*, AOL coproduced a "cybersimulcast," offering AOL members a unique window into the project with exclusive live coverage of the event and event participants. **www.aol.com**

 NETSCAPE Netscape Communications, a premier provider of open software for linking people and information, provided the Web browser and Web server software technology for all of the *24 Hours in Cyberspace* websites. The *24 Hours in Cyberspace* site uses the high-performance Netscape Communications Server and is optimized for viewing using Netscape Navigator. **www.netscape.com**

Silver Sponsors

 With the most advanced ATM network in the world, MFS Communications provided high-speed point-to-point and Internet connectivity, and all Centrex, local, and long-distance communications services for Mission Control, the publishing center for the project website. **www.mfst.com**

 Chosen by Apple as the first licensed manufacturer of MacOS compatibles, Power Computing manufactures and markets a full range of personal computer systems. For *24 Hours in Cyberspace*, Power Computing provided systems for Mission Control and for production of the book and CD-ROM. **www.powercc.com**

 ILLUSTRA Known as "the Database for Cyberspace," Illustra's multimedia database was the underlying management platform for all content associated with the *24 Hours in Cyberspace* website. **www.illustra.com**

 For *24 Hours in Cyberspace*, NEC Technologies' notebooks ensured that project photographers met their deadlines in remote locations around the world, while NEC monitors and personal computers helped Mission Control editors build the instant and permanent websites. **www.nec.com**

 NetObjects, a Bay Area startup, is building website development and management tools. The *24 Hours in Cyberspace* project used an early version of a NetObjects tool to build the entire site every 30 minutes, with all navigational links automatically updated. **www.netobjects.com**

 Studio Archetype (formerly known as Clement Mok designs) specializes in designing complex websites and designed the identity, structure, look and feel, and templates for the *24 Hours in Cyberspace* instant website. **www.cmdesigns.com**

A&I COLOR A&I is America's premier photographic laboratory, providing photographers with high-quality film processing and printing. The digital imaging services of A&I's sister company, ZZYZX Visual Systems, enables photographers to store, transmit, enhance, and reproduce their work. A&I provided the processing and duplication of all project film, and ZZYZX produced digital transparencies for the book. **www.zzyzxworld.com**

Major Contributors

Adaptive Solutions

Bay Networks

BBN Planet

Best Power

CE Software

Cisco Systems

Dallas Semiconductor

Digital Pond

Farallon Computing

FWB

Graham Technology Solutions

Herman Miller

Internet MCI

Internet World Exposition

MegaHertz

Newer Technology

NOW Software

Odwalla

Polaroid

Power Foods

Progressive Networks

San Francisco Hilton and Towers

The Software Construction
 Company

Sonic Solutions

Splash Technology

Teralinx Communications
 Corporation

Wildfire Communications

ZZYZX Visual Systems

Transmission Support

Advanced Laser Graphics

Artemis Research

Boston Photo Lab

Ken Hansen Imaging

San Francisco Examiner

The Seattle Times

Toppan Printing Co.

ZZYZX Visual Systems

Additional Support

Accel Partners

A.D.A.M. Software

A.G.E. Fotostock

The Agency

Al Bunetta Management

Aladdin Systems

Alex. Brown & Sons

Alliance Graphics

Ambrosia Software

American Photo Magazine

Applied Graphics Technology

Arent Fox Kintner Plotkin & Kahn

The Associated Press

Audio Video Technical Services

Balestra Capital

Barking Dog Builders

Big Fun Productions

The Big Idea Group

Big Software

Book Passage

The Brainerd Foundation

Carbone Smolan Associates

Cathay Pacific Airways

Citytv

Claris

A Clean Well Lighted Place
 for Books

Color 2000

Command Z

Contact Press Images

Creative Artists Agency

Cunningham Communications

Cyan

Cypress Club

Dae Advertising

Daedalus Books

The Depot Bookstore and Cafe

Disney Interactive

Dow, Lohnes & Albertson

Ellie Louise Catering

Environspec

Evan's Furniture

Event Security

Ex Machina

FPG International

General Magic

Germaines Restaurant

GNN

GRAF/x

H. Stockton Atlanta

The Hartsook Letter

Hi Fi

Holzmueller Productions

The Honolulu Advertiser

The Hopkins Bauman Group

HotWired

Howe-Lewis International

Hugh Lauter Levin Associates

Hummer Winblad Venture Partners

Ignition

Image Photographic Laboratory

Imagine Films

Institute for the Future

Integral Capital Partners

Interactive-8

Interval Research

Ion

Iuppa McCartan

Joe Boxer

Jones & Janello

Knowledge Adventure

Lecture Literary Management

Light Source

Lilien Productions

Living Books

Macadam

MacConnection

Macworld

Maine Photographic Workshop

Marin Independent Journal

McKinley Capital Partners

The McKinley Group

Media Synergy

Mercury Center

MetaTools

Mez Design

MFactory

Michael Rex Associates

M & M Distributing

Moon Handbooks

Moose's Restaurant

Morgan Stanley

Nash Editions

The New Lab

News Photographer Magazine

Nikon

NPPA

Ogilvy & Mather

On the Road Again Travel

The Oregonian

O'Reilly & Associates

Pallas Photo

Pathfinder

The Paul Allen Group

Peggy Kilburn Conference
 Management

Percepticon

Photo District News

Photo Perspectives

Pinacle Effects

Planet Out

Pop Rocket

Primal Screen

Proxima

Publishers Group West

Publishers Weekly

Qualex

Ready Set

Real World Studios

Remy Martin

Reportage

Rochester Institute of Technology

SanDisk

San Francisco Chronicle

San Francisco Examiner

Santa Fe Photographic Workshops

Sculley Communications

Seybold Seminars

Sheil Land Associates

Sheila Donnelly & Associates

Shiva Systems

Smithsonian Institute

Somerville House

Sony

Spider Island Software

Stanford Alumni Association

Star's Cafe

Starwave

Stockton Associates

Sygma Photos

Symantec

The Tattered Cover Book Store

TechArt

TED Conferences

Telex

Telos Systems

The Well

TonBo Designs

Tower Books

United Digital Artists

United Media

Unitel

Universal Press Syndicate

Upside Magazine

Visioneer

The Wall Street Journal

Waller Press

Walt Disney Imagineering

The Well

Worth Magazine

Xerox

Yahoo!

URL Road Map

Many of the stories in this book have related websites. Although website addresses change frequently, we've done our best to identify the most recent site associated with the stories below. All of these URLs are also included with the stories on the 24 Hours in Cyberspace website and CD-ROM. If you find that one of the URLs below no longer takes you to the related site, please visit the list of related sites on our website (http://www.cyber24.com/urls/), which is updated daily.

Human Touch

Page 21   Newcastle, Australia
  Email: cas@brushtail.hna.com.au
Page 22   Lusk, Wyoming, USA
  http://cassidy.wyoming.com/
Page 27   Austin, Texas, USA
  http://www.girlgamesinc.com/
Page 28   Charlotte, North Carolina, USA
  http://hwmin.gbgm-umc.org/CAM/memorials/johnsondh.html
Page 28   San Francisco, California, USA
  http://www.aidsquilt.org/
Page 31   Roxbury, Massachusetts, USA
  http://www.netdiva.com/isisplus.html
Page 32   Zagreb, Croatia
  http://www.geocities.com/WallStreet/3880/
  http://www.soros.org/
Page 32   Sarejevo, Bosnia
  http://web.cnam.fr/Sarajevo/zamir.html
Page 38   Phnom Penh, Cambodia
  http://grover.cecs.csulb.edu/~hing/genocide/
Page 38   Boston, Massachusetts, USA
  http://www.olywa.net/Deathrow/
Page 40   Tallin, Estonia
  http://www.csn.net/~era
Page 43   Yorkshire, England
  http://www.delphi.co.uk/delphi/wavey/
  http://www.compulink.co.uk/vip/waveydavey/Welcome.html
Page 44   Chadera, Israel
  http://www.ariga.com/peacebiz/peacelnk/recom.htm
Page 46   Blacksburg, Virginia, USA
  http://www.bev.net
Page 48   Swarthmore, Pennsylvania, USA
  http://www.links.net/

Earthwatch

Page 51   San Antonio, Texas, USA
  http://www.primenet.com/~skyblew/primar.html
Page 54   Wadi Natrun, Egypt
  Grand Haven, Michigan, USA
  http://www.scriptorium.org/scriptorium
Page 64   Westfield, England
  http://www.telescope.org/
Page 69   San Diego, California, USA
  http://k12.cnidr.org/gsh/gshwelcome.html
Page 70   Atlanta, Georgia, USA
  Beijing, China
  http://www.mecc.com/blueice.html
Page 73   Grotta degli Scogli Neri, Italy
  http://net.onion.it/speleoit/
Page 74   Manaus, Brazil
  http://www.cr-am.rnp.br/inpahome.html
Page 75   Angangueo, Mexico
  http://www.ties.k12.mn.us/~jnorth/jn-info.html
Page 76   Kenyir Lake, Malaysia
  http://www.si.edu/organiza/museums/zoo/homepage/zooview/crc/elephant/elephant.htm

Sex, Lies, and Websites

Page 90   Mountain View, California, USA
  http://www.glamazon.com/
Page 92   Denton, Texas, USA
  http://www.master.net/bryon
Page 93   Overland Park, Kansas, USA
  http://www.willa.com

Page 95   Toronto, Canada
  http://www.carolyn.org/~clburke/diary.html#
Page 96   Cambridge, Massachusetts, USA
  http://www-white.media.mit.edu/~steve/netcam.html
Page 97   New York, New York, USA
  http://www.cyberlove.com/free1.html
Page 98   Santa Cruz, California, USA
  http://www.darkwater.com
Page 99   San Francisco, California, USA
  http://www.cyborganic.com/
Page 100   Portland, Oregon, USA
  http://www.adultweb.com/licksisters/
Page 102   New York, New York, USA
  http://hamp.hampshire.edu/~temS95/hole.html
Page 103   Hollywood, California, USA
  http://www.nbc.com/entertainment/shows/homecourt/
Page 103   Vancouver, Canada
  http://www.xfiles.com/
  America Online keyword: XFILES
Page 105   Marina del Rey, California, USA
  http://www.thespot.com/
Page 105   Homewood, California, USA
  http://atlas.organic.com/atlas/multi/vixens
Page 106   Rio de Janeiro, Brazil
  http://www.redeglobo.com.br/
Page 109   Cybercafes Worldwide
  http://www.kokobar.com/IAC/IAC.html
Page 111   St. Petersburg, Russia
  Holmen, Wisconsin, USA
  http://www.arcom.spb.su/users/shade/
Page 114   South Lake Tahoe, Nevada, USA
  http://www.match.com/link.cgi/4631324004/welcome.tpl

Open for Business

Page 117   Carmel, Indiana, USA
  http://www.artline.com/
Page 119   San Carlos, California, USA
  http://www.ipp.com/ipp/tenadar/
Page 121   Cambridge, Massachusetts, USA
  http://www.w3.org/hypertext/WWW/People/Berners-Lee/
Page 123   Beverly Hills, California, USA
  http://www.planetout.com/
Page 124   Pasadena, California, USA
  http://www.hothothot.com
Page 125   Jeffersontown, Kentucky, USA
  http://www.iglou.com/dr_net/pets/petstuff.html
Page 126   Atlanta, Georgia, USA
  http://www.mermen.com/
Page 126   San Francisco, California, USA
  http://www.art.net/Music/HouseJacks/
Page 128   Singapore, Singapore
  http://www.ncb.gov.sg/lhh/
Page 129   Tokyo, Japan
  http://www.eccosys.com/PEOPLE/jito/
Page 136   New York, New York, USA
  http://www.finy.com/
Page 137   Upper Montclair, New Jersey, USA
  America Online keyword: NOVELIST
Page 138   Berryville, Virginia, USA
  http://www.presstar.com/fruitcake/aboutabb.html
Page 142   New York, New York, USA
  http://www.rga.com/
Page 143   Alexandria, Virginia, USA
  America Online keyword: MOTLEY FOOL

To the Rescue

Page 145   Dar es Salaam, Tanzania
  http://www.healthnet.org/
Page 147   Lancaster, Ohio, USA
  http://www.webcom.com/pleasant/sarah/teach/braille.html
Page 149   Somerville, Massachusetts, USA
  http://www.usa.net/welcome/saapage.html
Page 149   Oklahoma City, Oklahoma, USA
  http://www.uoknor.edu/okdaily/bombing.html
Page 153   Oklahoma City, Oklahoma, USA
  http://www.matmo.army.mil/
Page 154   Washington, D.C., USA
  http://www.matmo.army.mil/
Page 157   Maywood, Illinois, USA
  http://vhp.nus.sg/vhp/imagegal.html
Page 159   Mafinga, Tanzania
  http://vita.org/
Page 161   New York, New York, USA
  http://www.starbright.org/
Page 162   San Jose, California, USA
  http://www.detente.com/will/
Page 165   Charlottesville, Virginia, USA
  http://www.ew3.att.net/unos
Page 166   Fredericksburg, Virginia, USA
  Cairo, Egypt
  http://www.heroes.net/
Page 169   Peterson Air Force Base, Colorado, USA
  http://www.ceram.com/cheyenne/chey.html
Page 171   Victoria, Canada
  http://www.islandnet.com/deathnet/
Page 172   Windsor, Canada
  http://www.rights.org/~deathnet/HELP_AUSTIN.html
Page 174   San Jose, California, USA
  http://www.seniornet.com/
Page 175   Jerusalem, Israel
  http://www.netvision.net.il/php/harmony/index.html
Page 177   Ellicot City, Maryland, USA
  Moscow, Russia
  http://www.webcom.com/ica01/

Into the Light

Page 179   Port Alfred, South Africa
  Email: George@papanet.ru.ac.za
Page 180   Longreach, Australia
  http://www.qut.edu.au/
Page 183   Brooklyn, New York, USA
  http://www.chabad.org/
Page 185   Sheffield, England
  http://spacelink.msfc.nasa.gov/
Page 189   Kuala Lumpur, Malaysia
  http://smpke.jpm.my:1025/
Page 190   Washington, D.C., USA
  http://www.newshare.com:9999/moved.html
Page 190   San Francisco, California, USA
  http://www.hotwired.com/
  http://www.lambda.net/blue.html
Page 196   Kyushu, Japan
  http://www.network.or.jp/konjoin
Page 198   Vatican City, Italy
  http://www.vatican.va/
Page 200   Toronto, Canada
  http://www.webcom.com/~ezundel/english/welcome.html
Page 201   Nizkor Project
  http://www.almanac.bc.ca/
Page 205   Chiapas, Mexico
  http://www.peak.org/~justin/ezln/ezln.html
Page 207   Dharamsala, India
  http://www.manymedia.com/tibet/
  http://www.tibet.com/tibet.htm

On February 8, 1996, 40,000 people signed the walls of our "digital cave."

Look for your name and your friends on the end pages or visit our website at http://www.cyber24.com